How to Organize an Interactive Notebook

You may organize an interactive notebook in many different ways. You may choose to organize it by unit and work sequentially through the book. Or, you may choose to create different sections that you will revisit and add to throughout the year. Choose the format that works best for your students and subject.

An interactive notebook includes different types of pages in addition to the pages students create. Non-content pages you may want to add include the following:

Title Page

This page is useful for quickly identifying notebooks. It is especially helpful in classrooms that use multiple interactive notebooks for different subjects. Have students write the subject (such as "Math") on the title page of each interactive notebook. They should also include their full names. You may choose to have them include other information such as the teacher's name, classroom number, or class period.

Table of Contents

The table of contents is an integral part of the interactive notebook. It makes referencing previously created pages quick and easy for students. Make sure that students leave several pages at the beginning of each notebook for a table of contents.

Expectations and Grading Rubric

It is helpful for each student to have a copy of the expectations for creating interactive notebook pages. You may choose to include a list of expectations for parents and students to sign, as well as a grading rubric (page 11).

Unit Title Pages

Consider using a single page at the beginning of each section to separate it. Title the page with the unit name. Add a tab (page 78) to the edge of the page to make it easy to flip to the unit. Add a table of contents for only the pages in that unit.

Glossary

Reserve a six-page section at the back of the notebook where students can create a glossary. Draw a line to split in half the front and back of each page, creating 24 sections. Combine Q and R and Y and Z to fit the entire alphabet. Have students add an entry as each new vocabulary word is introduced.

What Type of Notebook Should I Use?

Spiral Notebook

The pages in this book are formatted for a standard one-subject notebook.

Pros

- Notebook can be folded in half.
- Page size is larger.
- It is inexpensive.
- It often comes with pockets for storing materials.

Cons

- Pages can easily fall out.
- Spirals can snag or become misshapen.
- Page count and size vary widely.
- It is not as durable as a binder.

Tips

- Encase the spiral in duct tape to make it more durable.
- Keep the notebooks in a central place to prevent them from getting damaged in desks.

Composition Notebook

Pros

- Pages don't easily fall out.
- Page size and page count are standard.
- It is inexpensive.

Cons

- Notebook cannot be folded in half.
- Page size is smaller.
- It is not as durable as a binder.

Tips

- Copy pages meant for standard-sized notebooks at 85 or 90 percent. Test to see which works better for your notebook.

Binder with Loose-Leaf Paper

Pros

- Pages can be easily added, moved, or removed.
- Pages can be removed individually for grading.
- You can add full-page printed handouts.
- It has durable covers.

Cons

- Pages can easily fall out.
- Pages aren't durable.
- It is more expensive than a notebook.
- Students can easily misplace or lose pages.
- Larger size makes it more difficult to store.

Tips

- Provide hole reinforcers for damaged pages.

Interactive Notebook Plan

Page	Topic	Page	Topic
1		51	
2		52	
3		53	
4		54	
5		55	
6		56	
7		57	
8		58	
9		59	
10		60	
11		61	
12		62	
13		63	
14		64	
15		65	
16		66	
17		67	
18		68	
19		69	
20		70	
21		71	
22		72	
23		73	
24		74	
25		75	
26		76	
27		77	
28		78	
29		79	
30		80	
31		81	
32		82	
33		83	
34		84	
35		85	
36		86	
37		87	
38		88	
39		89	
40		90	
41		91	
42		92	
43		93	
44		94	
45		95	
46		96	
47		97	
48		98	
49		99	
50		100	

Managing Interactive Notebooks in the Classroom

Working with Younger Students

- Use your yearly plan to preprogram a table of contents that you can copy and give to students to glue into their notebooks, instead of writing individual entries.

- Have assistants or parent volunteers precut pieces.

- Create glue sponges to make gluing easier. Place large sponges in plastic containers with white glue. The sponges will absorb the glue. Students can wipe the backs of pieces across the sponges to apply the glue with less mess.

Creating Notebook Pages

- For storing loose pieces, add a pocket to the inside back cover. Use the envelope pattern (page 81), an envelope, a jumbo library pocket, or a resealable plastic bag. Or, tape the bottom and side edges of the two last pages of the notebook together to create a large pocket.

- When writing under flaps, have students trace the outline of each flap so that they can visualize the writing boundary.

- Where the dashed line will be hidden on the inside of the fold, have students first fold the piece in the opposite direction so that they can see the dashed line. Then, students should fold the piece back the other way along the same fold line to create the fold in the correct direction.

- To avoid losing pieces, have students keep all of their scraps on their desks until they have finished each page.

- To contain paper scraps and avoid multiple trips to the trash can, provide small groups with small buckets or tubs.

- For students who run out of room, keep full and half sheets available. Students can glue these to the bottom of the pages and fold them up when not in use.

Dealing with Absences

- Create a model notebook for absent students to reference when they return to school.

- Have students cut a second set of pieces as they work on their own pages.

Using the Notebook

- To organize sections of the notebook, provide each student with a sheet of tabs (page 78).

- To easily find the next blank page, either cut off the top-right corner of each page as it is used or attach a long piece of yarn or ribbon to the back cover to be used as a bookmark.

What Are Interactive Notebooks?

Interactive notebooks are a unique form of note taking. Teachers guide students through creating pages of notes on new topics. Instead of being in the traditional linear, handwritten format, notes are colorful and spread across the pages. Notes also often include drawings, diagrams, and 3-D elements to make the material understandable and relevant. Students are encouraged to complete their notebook pages in ways that make sense to them. With this personalization, no two pages are exactly the same.

Because of their creative nature, interactive notebooks allow students to be active participants in their own learning. Teachers can easily differentiate pages to address the levels and needs of each learner. The notebooks are arranged sequentially, and students can create tables of contents as they create pages, making it simple for students to use their notebooks for reference throughout the year. The interactive, easily personalized format makes interactive notebooks ideal for engaging students in learning new concepts.

Using interactive notebooks can take as much or as little time as you like. Students will initially take longer to create pages but will get faster as they become familiar with the process of creating pages. You may choose to only create a notebook page as a class at the beginning of each unit, or you may choose to create a new page for each topic within a unit. You can decide what works best for your students and schedule.

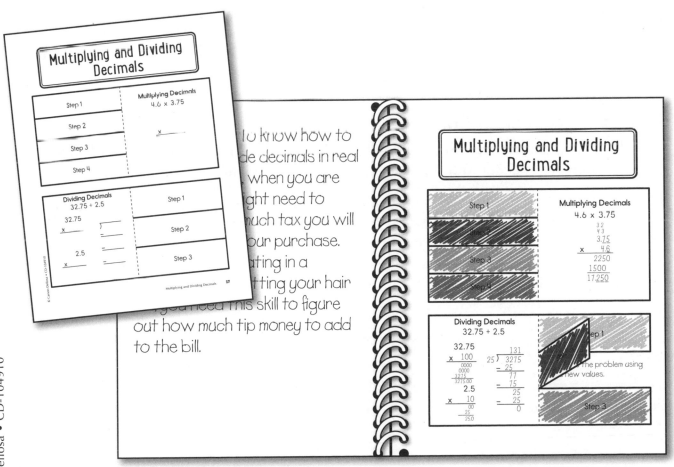

A student's interactive notebook for multiplying and dividing decimals

Getting Started

You can start using interactive notebooks at any point in the school year. Use the following guidelines to help you get started in your classroom. (For more specific details, management ideas, and tips, see page 10.)

1. Plan each notebook.

Use the planning template (page 9) to lay out a general plan for the topics you plan to cover in each notebook for the year.

2. Choose a notebook type.

Interactive notebooks are usually either single-subject, spiral-bound notebooks, composition books, or three-ring binders with loose-leaf paper. Each type presents pros and cons. See page 5 for a more in-depth look at each type of notebook.

3. Allow students to personalize their notebooks.

Have students decorate their notebook covers, as well as add their names and subjects. This provides a sense of ownership and emphasizes the personalized nature of the notebooks.

4. Number the pages and create the table of contents.

Have students number the bottom outside corner of each page, front and back. When completing a new page, adding a table of contents entry will be easy. Have students title the first page of each notebook "Table of Contents." Have them leave several blank pages at the front of each notebook for the table of contents. Refer to your general plan for an idea of about how many entries students will be creating.

5. Start creating pages.

Always begin a new page by adding an entry to the table of contents. Create the first notebook pages along with students to model proper format and expectations.

This book contains individual topics for you to introduce. Use the pages in the order that best fits your curriculum. You may also choose to alter the content presented to better match your school's curriculum. The provided lesson plans often do not instruct students to add color. Students should make their own choices about personalizing the content in ways that make sense to them. Encourage students to highlight and color the pages as they desire while creating them.

After introducing topics, you may choose to add more practice pages. Use the reproducibles (pages 78–96) to easily create new notebook pages for practice or to introduce topics not addressed in this book.

Use the grading rubric (page 11) to grade students' interactive notebooks at various points throughout the year. Provide students copies of the rubric to glue into their notebooks and refer to as they create pages.

Form

right ... and ... flat.
Th ... f the
sr ...

de

's on

:lude

ht

Planning for the Year

Making a general plan for interactive notebooks will help with planning, grading, and testing throughout the year. You do not need to plan every single page, but knowing what topics you will cover and in what order can be helpful in many ways.

Use the Interactive Notebook Plan (page 9) to plan your units and topics and where they should be placed in the notebooks. Remember to include enough pages at the beginning for the non-content pages, such as the title page, table of contents, and grading rubric. You may also want to leave a page at the beginning of each unit to place a mini table of contents for just that section.

In addition, when planning new pages, it can be helpful to sketch the pieces you will need to create. Use the following notebook template and notes to plan new pages.

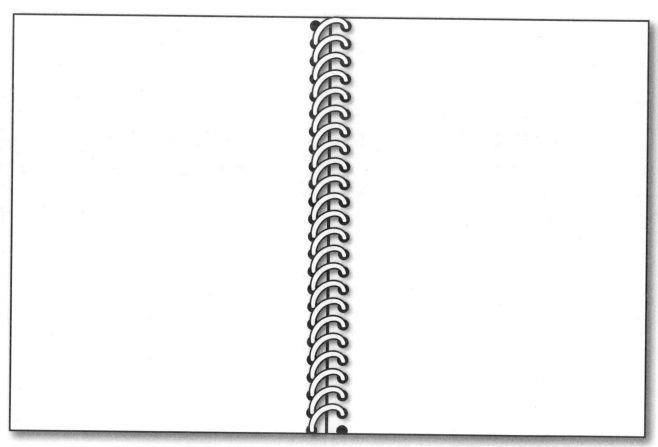

Left Side   **Right Side**

Notes

_____

_____

_____

Interactive Notebook Grading Rubric

4

_____ Table of contents is complete.

_____ All notebook pages are included.

_____ All notebook pages are complete.

_____ Notebook pages are neat and organized.

_____ Information is correct.

_____ Pages show personalization, evidence of learning, and original ideas.

3

_____ Table of contents is mostly complete.

_____ One notebook page is missing.

_____ Notebook pages are mostly complete.

_____ Notebook pages are mostly neat and organized.

_____ Information is mostly correct.

_____ Pages show some personalization, evidence of learning, and original ideas.

2

_____ Table of contents is missing a few entries.

_____ A few notebook pages are missing.

_____ A few notebook pages are incomplete.

_____ Notebook pages are somewhat messy and unorganized.

_____ Information has several errors.

_____ Pages show little personalization, evidence of learning, or original ideas.

1

_____ Table of contents is incomplete.

_____ Many notebook pages are missing.

_____ Many notebook pages are incomplete.

_____ Notebook pages are too messy and unorganized to use.

_____ Information is incorrect.

_____ Pages show no personalization, evidence of learning, or original ideas.

Multi-Digit Division

Introduction

Write $6\overline{)96}$ and $8\overline{)216}$ on the board. Have students work with partners to solve each problem. Discuss the various strategies that were used to solve each problem.

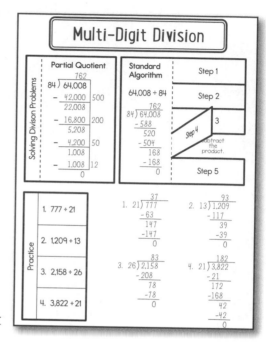

Creating the Notebook Page

Guide students through the following steps to complete the right-hand page in their notebooks.

1. Add a Table of Contents entry for the Multi-Digit Division pages.

2. Cut out the title and glue it to the top of the page.

3. Cut out the *Partial Quotient* and *Area Models* flaps. Apply glue to the gray glue section of the *Area Models* flap and place the *Partial Quotient* flap on top of it so that the left flaps align. Apply glue to the back of the left section of the flap book and attach it to the top left side of the page.

4. On each flap, show step-by-step examples of how to use each strategy for multi-digit division. Under the *Area Models* flap, note any helpful information about each strategy.

5. Cut out the *Standard Algorithm* flap book. Cut on the solid lines to create five flaps. Apply glue to the back of the left section and attach it the top right side of the page.

6. Under each flap, write a description of the step. (Step 1: Rewrite the problem if necessary. Step 2: Divide the first part of the dividend by a one-digit number. Step 3: Write the product under the first part of the dividend. Step 4: Subtract the product. Step 5: Drop down the next part of the dividend and repeat the process until the quotient is found.)

7. Solve the example problem. If desired, color code the flaps and each step of the process to match.

8. Cut out the *Practice* piece and glue it to the bottom left side of the page.

9. Use the standard algorithm to solve each problem on the right side of the page.

Reflect on Learning

To complete the left-hand page, have students use all three strategies to solve $22\overline{)7128}$ and explain which strategy they prefer and why.

Answer Key:
1. 37; 2. 93; 3. 83; 4. 182

Multi-Digit Division

Practice

1. 777 ÷ 21

2. 1,209 ÷ 13

3. 2,158 ÷ 26

4. 3,822 ÷ 21

Standard Algorithm

64,008 ÷ 84

Step 1

Step 2

Step 3

Step 4

Step 5

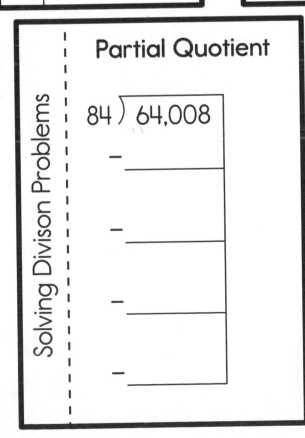

Partial Quotient

Solving Divison Problems

84) 64,008

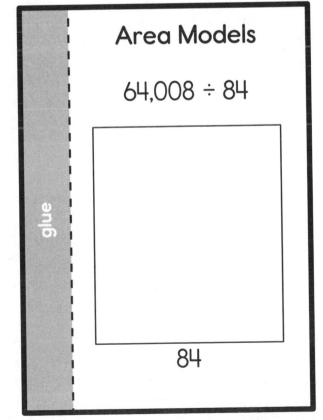

Area Models

64,008 ÷ 84

glue

84

Adding and Subtracting Decimals

Review adding multi-digit numbers by aligning digits with regard to place value. Write *234 + 46* on the board in a vertical format with the first digit of each number aligned. Ask students why an addition problem cannot be solved in this way. Have students work with partners to explain and share ideas with the class.

Creating the Notebook Page

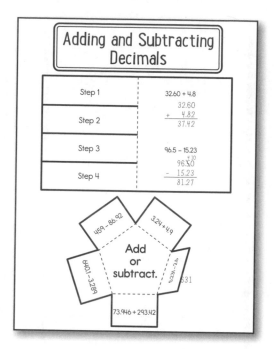

Guide students through the following steps to complete the right-hand page in their notebooks.

1. Add a Table of Contents entry for the Adding and Subtracting Decimals pages.

2. Cut out the title and glue it to the top of the page.

3. Cut out the rectangular flap book. Cut on the solid lines to create four flaps. Apply glue to the back of the right section and attach it below the title.

4. Under each flap, write a description of the step. (1. Line up decimals vertically. 2. Add a zero to the end (after the decimal) if necessary. 3. Beginning with the lowest place value, add or subtract from right to left. 4. Bring down the decimal.)

5. Solve the example problem. If desired, color code the flaps and each step of the process to match.

6. Cut out the *Add or* flap book. Apply glue to the back of the pentagon-shaped center section and attach it to the bottom of the page.

7. Solve each problem and write the sum or difference under the flap.

Reflect on Learning

To complete the left-hand page, have students create two decimal numbers using the digits from their birthdays and other common numbers such as a lunch number or phone number. Then, they should use the numbers they create to model both an addition and subtraction problem using the four steps.

Answer Key
Clockwise from top right: 8.14; 2.631; 367.366; 636.811; 372.08

Adding and Subtracting Decimals

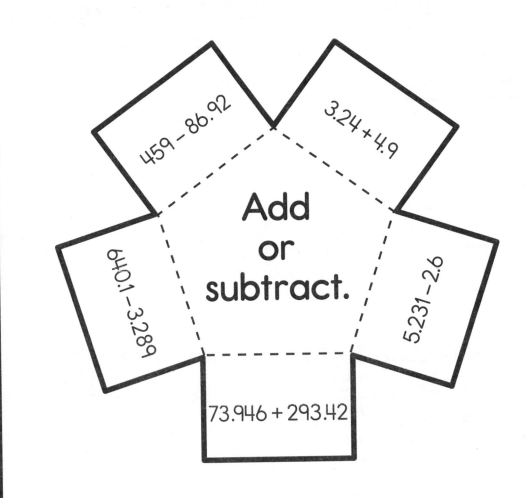

459 – 86.92

3.24 + 4.9

Add or subtract.

640.1 – 3.289

5.231 – 2.6

73.946 + 293.42

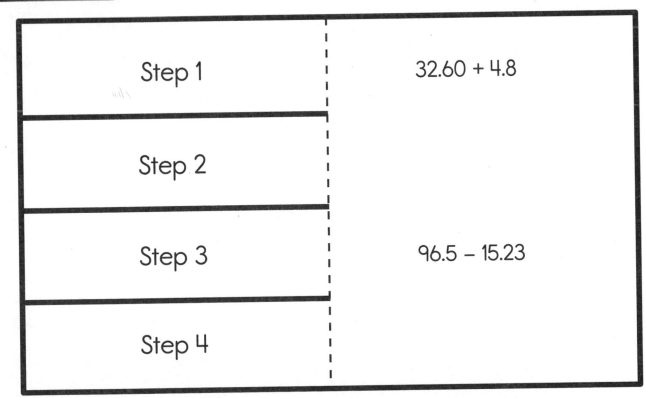

Step 1	32.60 + 4.8
Step 2	
Step 3	96.5 – 15.23
Step 4	

Multiplying and Dividing Decimals

Introduction

Review the standard algorithm for multiplying multi-digit numbers by writing *35 × 76* on the board. Students should solve the problem and then explain how they solved it. Then, review the parts of a division problem by writing *15 ÷ 3 = 5* on the board. Students should label the numbers in the problem with *dividend, divisor,* and *quotient.*

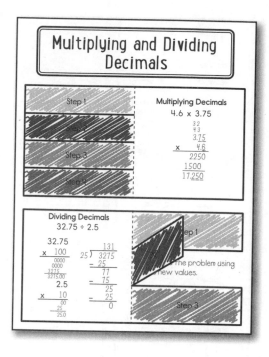

Creating the Notebook Page

Guide students through the following steps to complete the right-hand page in their notebooks.

1. Add a Table of Contents entry for the Multiplying and Dividing Decimals pages.

2. Cut out the title and glue it to the top of the page.

3. Cut out the *Multiplying Decimals* flap book. Cut on the solid lines to create four flaps. Apply glue to the back of the right section and attach it below the title.

4. Under each flap, write a description of the step. (1. Line up the last digit of each number vertically. 2. Use the standard algorithm to multiply the numbers. 3. Count to find the total number of digits after the decimals in the problem. 4. Count from right to left the same number of places to add a decimal to the product.)

5. Color each flap a different color. Then, solve the example problem and color code each step of the process to match the flaps.

3. Cut out the *Dividing Decimals* flap book. Cut on the solid lines to create three flaps. Apply glue to the back of the left section and attach it to the bottom of the page.

4. Under each flap, write a description of the step. (1. Multiply both the divisor and dividend by a power of 10 to remove the decimal from the divisor. 2. Rewrite the problem using the new values. 3. Find the quotient.)

5. Color each flap a different color. Then, solve the example problem and color code each step of the process to match the flaps.

Reflect on Learning

To complete the left-hand page, have students think of a real-life situation when it would be necessary to use multiplication or division of decimals. Then, they should explain each situation.

Multiplying and Dividing Decimals

Step 1	Multiplying Decimals
Step 2	4.6 x 3.75
Step 3	x _____
Step 4	

Dividing Decimals	Step 1
32.75 ÷ 2.5	
32.75	Step 2
x _____	
2.5	Step 3
x _____	

Greatest Common Factor and Least Common Multiple

Each student will need a brass paper fastener to complete this page.

Introduction

Review factors and multiples. Explain that factors are numbers that divide evenly into a number. Have students work with partners to list the factors of 24 (1, 2, 3, 4, 6, 8, 12, 24). Then, explain that to find multiples of a number, they must multiply the number by another number. Have students work with partners to find the first five multiples of 8 (8, 16, 24, 32, 40).

Creating the Notebook Page

Guide students through the following steps to complete the right-hand page in their notebooks.

1. Add a Table of Contents entry for the Greatest Common Factor and Least Common Multiple pages.

2. Cut out the title and glue it to the top of the page.

3. Cut out the rectangle with the definitions. Fold in on the dashed line to create a book. Apply glue to the back of the book and attach it to the top left the page.

4. Write *Definitions* on the front of the book. Complete the sentences in the book. (The **Greatest** Common **Factor** is the largest **magnitude** number that can **divide** two numbers. The **Least** Common **Multiple** is the **smallest** quantity that is a **multiple** of **two** or more numbers.)

5. Cut out the circles and place the smaller numbered circle on top of the large circle. Place the gray glue circle on the bottom with the gray side facing out. Push a brass paper fastener through the center of the circles to attach them. It may be helpful to create a hole in each piece separately first. Apply glue to the gray glue section. Attach it to the top right of the page. Do not press the brass paper fastener through the page. Both number circles should spin freely.

6. Cut out the four-column table and glue it to the bottom of the page.

7. Spin the number circles to create four number combinations. Write them on the table. Then, find the greatest common factor and least common multiple for each combination.

Greatest Common Factor and Least Common Multiple

Definitions

First Number	Second Number	Greatest Common Factor	Least Common Multiple
8	4	2	8
20	15	5	60
14	6	2	42
9	12	3	36

Reflect on Learning

To complete the left-hand page, find the least common multiple between your age and your grade level. Then, find the greatest common factor between your age and your math teacher's room number. Explain how you found both answers.

18

The spinner wheels:

15, 6, 4, 18, 12, 21

8, 20, 16, 9, 14, 10

glue

Greatest Common Factor and Least Common Multiple

The _____ Common _____ is the largest _____ number that can _____ two numbers.

The _____ Common _____ is the _____ quantity that is a _____ of _____ or more numbers.

First Number	Second Number	Greatest Common Factor	Least Common Multiple

The Distributive Property

Write 8 × (4 +2) on the board. Have students work with partners to solve the problem using order of operations. Explain that the distributive property can also be used to solve similar problems.

Creating the Notebook Page

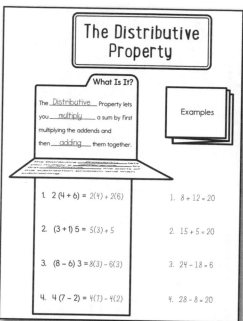

Guide students through the following steps to complete the right-hand page in their notebooks.

1. Add a Table of Contents entry for the The Distributive Property pages.

2. Cut out the title and glue it to the top of the page.

3. Cut out the *What Is It?* mini file folder. Fold it in half on the dashed line. Apply glue to the back and attach it to the top left side of the page.

4. Complete the sentences in the mini file folder. (The **Distributive** Property lets you **multiply** a sum by first multiplying the addends and then **adding** them together. The Distributive **Property** lets you multiply a **difference** by first **multiplying** the parts of the **subtraction** problem and then subtracting.)

4. Cut out the accordion fold piece. Starting with the end that says *Examples*, fold the pieces back and forth to create an accordion with *Examples* on top. Apply glue to the back of the last flap and attach it to the top right side of the page.

5. Show how each of the examples can be rewritten to use the distributive property.

6. Cut out the numbered rectangle and glue it to the left side of the bottom of the page.

7. Rewrite each problem using the distributive property. Then, solve it. Show your work on the right side of the page.

Reflect on Learning

To complete the left-hand page, have students explain why the distributive property is helpful in solving math problems.

Answer Key
1. 20; 2. 20; 3. 6; 4. 20

Examples

$$a(b+c) =$$

$$a(b-c) =$$

$$(b+c)\,a =$$

$$(b-c)\,a =$$

The Distributive Property

What Is It?

The _____ Property lets you _____ a sum by first multiplying the addends and then _____ them together.

The Distributive _____ lets you multiply a _____ by first _____ the parts of the subtraction problem and then subtracting.

1. $2(4+6) =$

2. $(3+1)\,5 =$

3. $(8-6)\,3 =$

4. $4(7-2) =$

Dividing Fractions

Review how to multiply fractions by using an array model and by using the standard algorithm. Write $\frac{2}{4} \times \frac{3}{5}$ on the board. Have students show how to find the product using each method.

Creating the Notebook Page

Guide students through the following steps to complete the right-hand page in their notebooks.

1. Add a Table of Contents entry for the Dividing Fractions pages.

2. Cut out the title and glue it to the top of the page.

3. Complete the sentence under the title. (When **dividing** fractions, you are finding out how many of one **fraction** are **equal** to **another** fraction.)

4. Draw two vertical lines to divide the middle of the page into a 3-column chart. Cut out the three fraction problems and glue them in the left column, leaving space between each problem.

5. Cut out the fraction bars and glue them in pairs in the middle column to match the fractions in each problem.

6. Shade in the fraction bars so that the shaded parts match the fractions in each problem.

7. To solve each problem, write how many portions of the divisor are in the dividend in the third column.

8. Cut out the accordion fold. Starting with the arrow end, fold the pieces back and forth to create an accordion with the arrow on top. Apply glue to the back of the last flap and attach it to the bottom left side of the page. Shade the triangle a different color so it stands out from the pieces behind it.

9. Cut out the flap book. Cut on the solid lines to create three flaps. Apply glue to the back of the top section and attach it to the bottom right side of the page.

10. Using the steps on the accordion fold, solve each division problem under the flap.

Reflect on Learning

To complete the left-hand page, have students create a rhyming verse to help them remember the steps for using the standard algorithm to divide fractions.

Answer Key
$\frac{1}{9}$; 4; 2

22

Dividing Fractions

When _____ fractions, you are finding out how many of one _____ are _____ to _____ fraction.

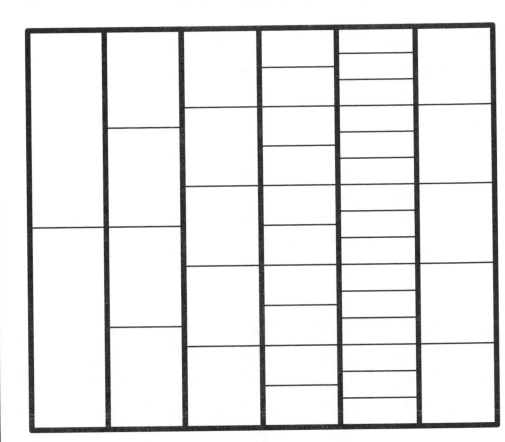

$$\frac{1}{15} \div \frac{3}{5} \qquad \frac{2}{5} \div \frac{1}{10} \qquad \frac{1}{2} \div \frac{1}{4}$$

1. Change the divisor to the reciprocal fraction.

2. Change the operation to multiplication.

3. Solve the problem.

How to Divide Fractions

Divide.

$$\frac{1}{15} \div \frac{3}{5} \qquad \frac{2}{5} \div \frac{1}{10} \qquad \frac{1}{2} \div \frac{1}{4}$$

Positive and Negative Numbers

Introduction

Place a number line on the board that runs from 0 to 10. Ask students if they have ever heard a weather forecast that predicts a temperature that is "below zero." Have students explain what they think it means when a temperature is "below zero."

Creating the Notebook Page

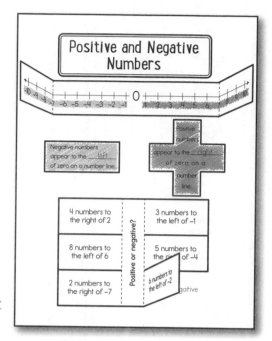

Guide students through the following steps to complete the right-hand page in their notebooks.

1. Add a Table of Contents entry for the Positive and Negative Numbers pages.

2. Cut out the title and glue it to the top of the page.

3. Cut out the number line. Fold in on the dashed lines. Apply glue to the back of the center section and place it below the title.

4. Use one color to highlight the numbers to the right of zero on the number line. Use another color to highlight the numbers to the left of zero on the number line.

5. Cut out the addition and subtraction symbols. Glue the addition symbol below the number line to the right and the subtraction symbol below the number line to the left.

6. Complete the sentences on the symbols. (Positive numbers appear to the **right** of zero on a number line. Negative numbers appear to the **left** of zero on a number line.)

7. Color the addition sign using the same color you used for the numbers to the right of zero. Color the subtraction symbol using the same color you used for the numbers to the left of zero.

8. Cut out the flap book. Cut on the solid lines to create three flaps on each side. Apply glue to the back of the center section and attach it to the bottom of the page.

9. Write *positive* or *negative* under each flap to indicate which type of number is described on the flap.

Reflect on Learning

To complete the left-hand page, have students write examples of two or three real-life negative numbers (other than the example given in the Introduction) and explain how they are used.

Positive and Negative Numbers

Positive numbers appear to the _____ of zero on a number line.

Negative numbers appear to the _____ of zero on a number line.

	Positive or negative?	
4 numbers to the right of 2		3 numbers to the left of –1
8 numbers to the left of 6		5 numbers to the right of –4
2 numbers to the right of –7		6 numbers to the left of –2

Absolute Value

Review positive and negative numbers by drawing a blank number line on the board. Distribute to students a selection of positive and negative numbers written on index cards. Then, have students place themselves across the front of the room as they would fall on the number line.

Creating the Notebook Page

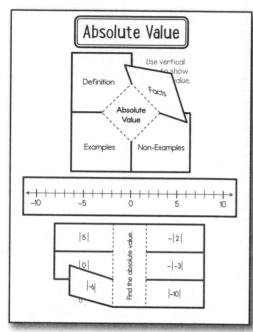

Guide students through the following steps to complete the right-hand page in their notebooks.

1. Add a Table of Contents entry for the Absolute Value pages.

2. Cut out the title and glue it to the top of the page.

3. Cut out the *Absolute Value* flap book. Cut on the solid lines to create four flaps. Apply glue to the back of the center section and attach it to the page below the title.

4. Under each flap, take notes about absolute value. (Definition: the distance a number is from zero; Facts: use vertical bars to show absolute value, $|x|$; Examples: $|7| = 7$, $|-7| = 7$, $-|7| = -7$, $-|-7| = -7$; Non-examples: $-\frac{1}{2}$, -8, 2)

5. Cut out the number line and glue it below the square.

6. Cut out the *Find the absolute* flap book. Cut along the solid lines to create three flaps on each side. Apply glue to back of the center section and attach it to the bottom of the page.

7. Use the number line to solve each problem. Write the answers under the flaps.

Reflect on Learning

To complete the left-hand page, students should choose one value and represent it with absolute value in multiple ways. Then, have students explain why the absolute value of a negative number results in a positive number. Finally, have students explain why the negative value of an absolute value results in a negative number.

Answer Key
Left Column: 5; 0; 6; Right Column: −2; −3; 10

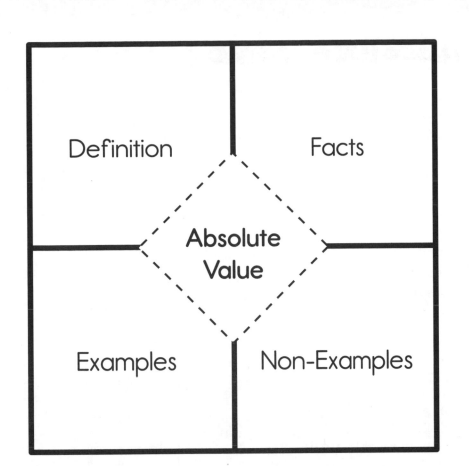

Definition	Facts

Absolute Value

Examples	Non-Examples

Absolute Value

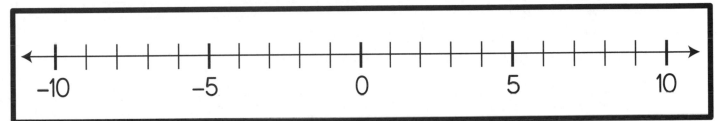

-10   -5   0   5   10

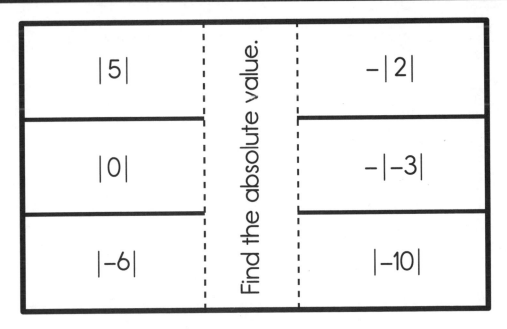

$|5|$	Find the absolute value.	$-|2|$
$|0|$		$-|-3|$
$|-6|$		$|-10|$

Integers in the Coordinate Plane

Introduction

Draw a coordinate grid on the board with the positive x- and y-axes. Mark the following points: *A* at (2, 3); *B* at (4, 2); and *C* at (1, 6). Have students work with partners to name the ordered pairs for each point.

Creating the Notebook Page

Guide students through the following steps to complete the right-hand page in their notebooks.

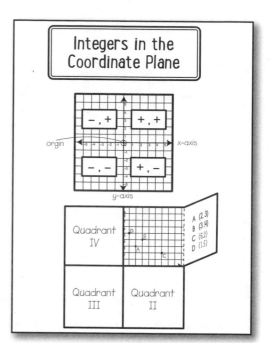

1. Add a Table of Contents entry for the Integers in the Coordinate Plane pages.

2. Cut out the title and glue it to the top of the page.

3. Cut out the coordinate grid and glue it below the title.

4. Label the part: *x-axis*, *y-axis*, and *origin*.

5. Cut out the four small integer labels. Glue each one in the quadrant that matches the integer symbols on the label.

6. Cut out the large grid flap book. Cut on the solid lines to create four flaps. Fold the flaps in on the dashed lines. Apply glue to the back of the center section and attach it to the bottom of the page.

7. Mark and label the points *A, B, E, F, I, J, M*, and *N* on the coordinate grid. Then, write the ordered pairs for points *C, D, G, H, K, L, O*, and *P*.

8. Fold in each flap and label the quadrants: *I, II, III, IV*

Reflect on Learning

To complete the left-hand page, have students explain how using a coordinate plane can be helpful in real life.

Answer Key

1. C: (6, 2); D: (1, 5); G: (2, −1); H: (5, −4); K: (−1, 2); L: (−3, 1); O: (−1, −3); P: (−2, −1)

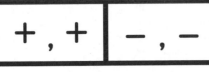

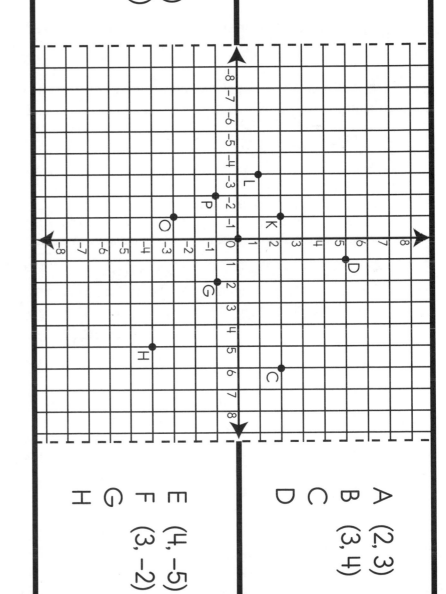

Integers in the Coordinate Plane

I (–5, 4)
J (–7, 8)
K
L

M (–4, –4)
N (–6, –5)
O
P

A (2, 3)
B (3, 4)
C
D

E (4, –5)
F (3, –2)
G
H

Ratios

Introduction

Pose this situation to students: *A bird nest has three baby birds in it. How many wings and beaks are in the nest altogether?* Call on students for responses. Write 6:3 on the board. Then, explain that when the number of wings and beaks in the nest are compared, a ratio is created.

Creating the Notebook Page

Guide students through the following steps to complete the right-hand page in their notebooks.

1. Add a Table of Contents entry for the Ratios pages.

2. Cut out the title and glue it to the top of the page.

3. Complete the definition (a **comparison** of **two** or more **numbers**).

4. Cut out the flap book. Glue it to the top of the page.

5. Fill in the blanks to complete the examples. (There are **6** circles to **4** squares; **6:4**; $\frac{6}{4}$; **6** to **4**)

6. Select a number of circles and color them blue. Then, select a number of squares and color them red. Under the flaps, write the new ratios of blue circles to red squares.

7. Cut out the four accordion folds. Starting at the end with pictures, fold each piece back and forth to create an accordion fold with the picture on top. Apply glue to the back of the last flap and attach each piece to the bottom of the page in a 2 × 2 arrangement.

8. Use the pictures to complete the ratio statement on each accordion fold. Then, on the blank folds of the accordion fold, show how to write the ratio three different ways.

Reflect on Learning

To complete the left-hand page, have students think of two real-life situations and create ratios to explain those situations. Students should describe the situations using ratio language.

Answer Key

3 stars, 2 triangles, 3:2, $\frac{3}{2}$, 3 to 2; 5 U's, 3 T's, 5:3, $\frac{5}{3}$, 5 to 3; 5 squares, 6 triangles, 5:6, $\frac{5}{6}$, 5 to 6; 4 boys, 3 girls, 4:3, $\frac{4}{3}$, 4 to 3

Ratios

a ____ of ____ or more

There are ____ circles to ____ squares.

____ : ____

——

____ to ____

There are ____ ____ to ____ ____.

There are ____ ____ to ____ ____.

There are ____ ____ to ____ ____.

There are ____ ____ to ____ ____.

Solving Ratios

Introduction

Pose this situation to students: *Joseph practices the trumpet for 2 hours each day.* Write the ratio *2:1* on the board. Have students determine how many hours Joseph practices over two, three, and five days. Then, write to show that they are equivalent ratios.

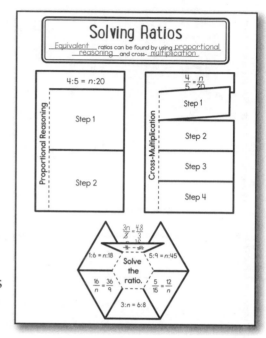

Creating the Notebook Page

Guide students through the following steps to complete the right-hand page in their notebooks.

1. Add a Table of Contents entry for the Solving Ratios pages.

2. Cut out the title and glue it to the top of the page.

3. Complete the sentence under the title. (**Equivalent** ratios can be found by using **proportional reasoning** or cross-**multiplication**.)

4. Cut out the *Porportional Reasoning* flap book. Cut on the solid lines to create two flaps. Apply glue to the back of the left and top sections and attach it to the top left side of the page.

5. Write the steps for using proportional reasoning to solve ratios on the back of each flap. (Step 1: Find the factor that allows one value in the known ratio to be converted to the known value in the unknown ratio. Step 2: Multiply it by the other value in the known ratio.) Under each flap, show how to use the steps to solve the example problem.

6. Cut out the *Cross-Multiplication* flap book. Cut on the solid lines to create four flaps. Apply glue to the back of the left and top sections and attach it to the top right side of the page.

7. Write the steps for using cross-multiplication to solve ratios on the back of each flap. (Step 1: Set up as a cross-multiplication problem. Step 2: Multiply each set of values. Step 3: Use division to isolate the unknown value. Step 4: Solve the problem.) Then, show how to use the steps under each flap to solve the example problem.

8. Cut out the hexagon flap book. Apply glue to the back of the center section and attach it to the bottom of the page. Solve each ratio and write the answer under the flap.

Reflect on Learning

To complete the left-hand page, have students solve an equivalent ratios word problem: *Three hours into a snowstorm, 2 inches of snow has fallen. If snow continues to fall for 6 more hours, how many inches of snow will fall altogether?* Have students solve and explain how they used ratios to find the answer.

Answer Key
Clockwise from top: 16; 25; 36; 4; 4; 3

© Carson-Dellosa • CD-104910

Solving Ratios

_____ ratios can be found by using _____
_____ and cross-_____.

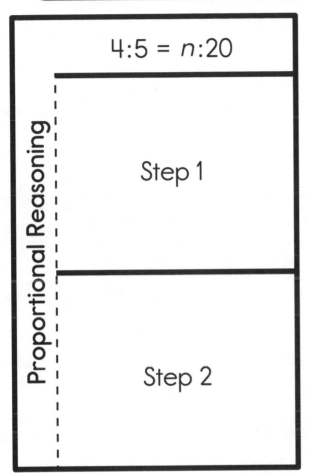

Proportional Reasoning

$4:5 = n:20$

Step 1

Step 2

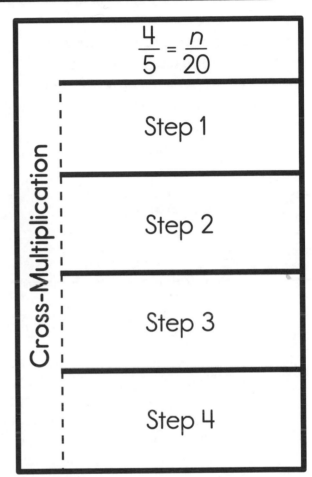

Cross-Multiplication

$\dfrac{4}{5} = \dfrac{n}{20}$

Step 1

Step 2

Step 3

Step 4

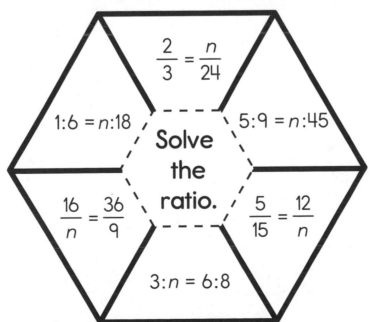

$\dfrac{2}{3} = \dfrac{n}{24}$

$1:6 = n:18$

$5:9 = n:45$

Solve the ratio.

$\dfrac{16}{n} = \dfrac{36}{9}$

$\dfrac{5}{15} = \dfrac{12}{n}$

$3:n = 6:8$

Unit Rates

Introduction

Review ratios by writing $\frac{3}{4}$ on the board. Have students discuss multiple meanings of the ratio and what it could possibly represent.

Creating the Notebook Page

Guide students through the following steps to complete the right-hand page in their notebooks.

1. Add a Table of Contents entry for the Unit Rates pages.

2. Cut out the title and glue it to the top of the page.

3. Complete the definition. (A unit **rate** is a **ratio** for **one** unit.)

4. Cut out the two-column flap. Apply glue to the back of the top section and attach it to the top left side of the page.

5. Under the flap, find the unit rate and explain how you found your answer.

6. Cut out the *Examples* piece on the solid lines. Fold and unfold the piece on the three dashed lines. With the piece oriented so that the folds form an X with a horizontal line through it, pull the left and right sides together at the fold line. Then, keeping the sides touching, bring the top edge down to meet the bottom edge. You should be left with a triangular shape that unfolds into a square. Apply glue to the back of the triangle to attach it to the right side of the page below the title.

7. Unfold the *Examples* piece. Brainstorm additional examples of unit rates inside the square.

8. Cut out the *What is the best buy?* triangles. Apply glue to the back of the center triangles and attach them to the bottom of the page.

9. Find the unit rate for each price described and write the rate under each flap. Then, color the flap that represents the best buy on each triangle.

Reflect on Learning

To complete the left-hand page, have students think of a school supply they buy each year. Have students research prices from two or three sources and find the one that offers the best unit rate.

Answer Key
Boneless Chicken (clockwise from top left): $5.00 per 1 pound; $5.00 per 1 pound; $4.00 per 1 pound; Fruit Punch (clockwise from top left): $6\frac{2}{5}$ ounces per dollar; 8 ounces per dollar; $5\frac{1}{3}$ ounces per dollar

Unit Rates

A unit _____ is a _____ for _____ unit.

Miles Walked	Time (hours)
6	2
9	3
15	5
21	7

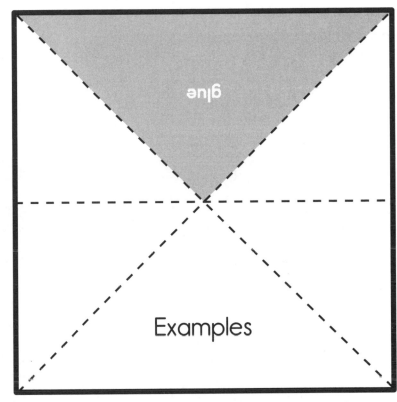

glue

Examples

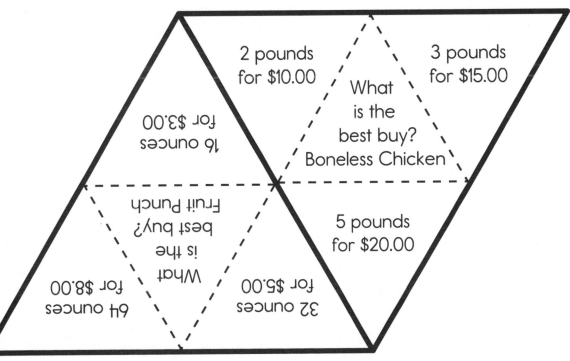

2 pounds for $10.00

3 pounds for $15.00

What is the best buy? Boneless Chicken

16 ounces for $3.00

5 pounds for $20.00

Fruit Punch best buy? is the What

32 ounces for $5.00

64 ounces for $8.00

Percents

Introduction

Review finding equivalent fractions and ratios. Write $\frac{2}{3}$ on the board. Have students create visual representations showing $\frac{2}{3}$ and then further divide their visual representation to find at least three equivalent fractions.

Creating the Notebook Page

Guide students through the following steps to complete the right-hand page in their notebooks.

1. Add a Table of Contents entry for the Percents pages.

2. Cut out the title and glue it to the top of the page.

3. Complete the definition of *percent*. (A **percent** is a **ratio** that compares a **number** to **100**.)

4. Cut out the rectangle with the large grid and glue it below the title.

5. Shade the grid to show the fraction. Complete the missing spaces to show how to find a percent when given a fraction.

6. Cut out the 10-flap shutter fold. Cut on the solid lines to create five flaps on each side. Apply glue to the gray glue area and attach it to the bottom of the page. Fold the flaps in over the center.

7. Given the fraction on each flap, show the visual representation using the hundred grid. Show the equivalent fraction given 100 as the denominator and the equivalent percent under the flaps for each fraction.

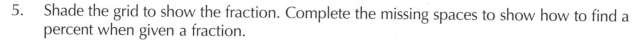

Reflect on Learning

To complete the left-hand page, have students explain three situations when solving percents is helpful in real-life.

Answer Key

$\frac{70}{100}$; 70%; $\frac{50}{100}$; 50%; $\frac{75}{100}$; 75%; $\frac{40}{100}$; 40%; $\frac{68}{100}$; 68%

Percents

A _____ is a _____ that compares a _____ to _____.

$$\frac{4}{5} = \frac{?}{100} = \quad = \frac{}{100} = \quad \%$$

$\frac{1}{5}$ $\frac{1}{5}$ $\frac{1}{5}$ $\frac{1}{5}$ $\frac{1}{5}$

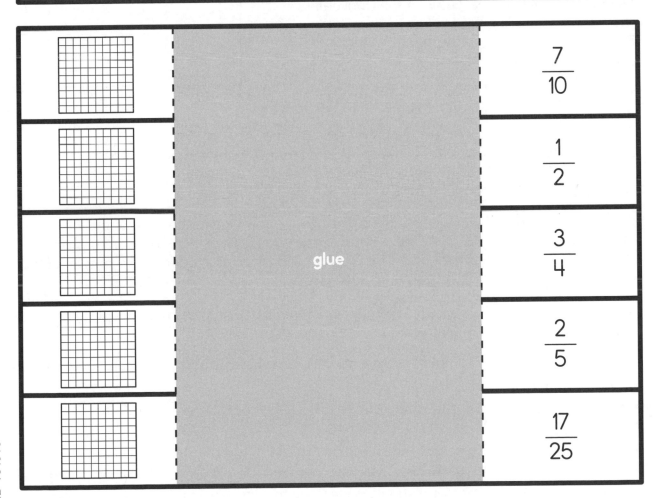

$\frac{7}{10}$

$\frac{1}{2}$

glue

$\frac{3}{4}$

$\frac{2}{5}$

$\frac{17}{25}$

Converting Measurements Using Ratios

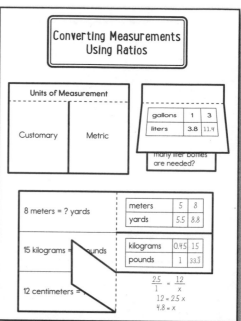

Introduction

Review converting measurements within the customary measurement system by writing *12 inches = 1 foot* and *3 feet = 1 yard* on the board. Have students explain how to figure out how many inches are in 4 feet. Explain that students can use the same process to convert between customary and metric measurement systems if the values to use are known.

Creating the Notebook Page

Guide students through the following steps to complete the right-hand page in their notebooks.

1. Add a Table of Contents entry for the Converting Measurements Using Ratios pages.

2. Cut out the title and glue it to the top of the page.

3. Cut out the *Units of Measurement* flap book. Cut on the solid line to create two flaps. Apply glue to the back of the top flap and attach it to the left of the page below the title.

4. Below the flaps, take notes about the approximate conversions. (Some examples are: 2.5 centimeters ≈ 1 inch; 5.5 yards ≈ 5 meters; 1 mile ≈ 1.6 kilometers; 1 gallon ≈ 3.8 liters; 1 pound ≈ 0.45 kilograms)

5. Cut out the word problem piece and the chart flap. Apply glue to the back of the top section of the chart flap and attach it to the right of the flap book. Then, glue the word problem under the chart flap. Solve the example problem and show your work on the bottom of the flap. (3.8 x 3 = 11.4, 12 liter bottles are needed)

6. Cut out the *8 meters* flap book. Cut on the solid lines to create three flaps. Apply glue to the back of the left section and attach it to the bottom of the page.

7. Solve each problem by completing the ratio table on each flap. Show the math for each ratio under each flap.

Reflect on Learning

To complete the left-hand page, have students think of several real-life situations when they would need to use a number form conversion. Students should write three real-life word problems for a classmate to solve and include an answer key.

Answer Key
8.8 yards; 33.33 pounds; 4.8 inches

Converting Measurements Using Ratios

gallons	1	3
liters	3.8	

3 gallons of soda are needed to make punch, but it is only sold in liter bottles. How many liter bottles are needed?

Units of Measurement

Customary	Metric

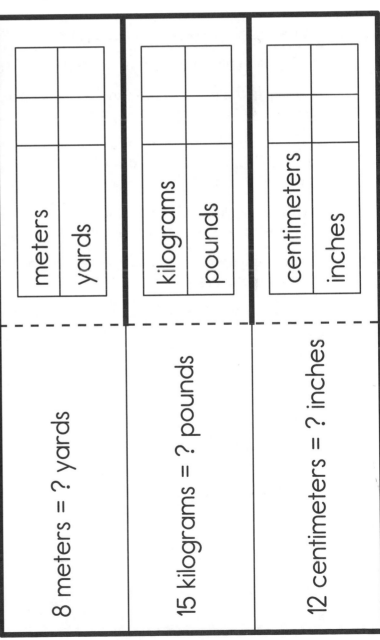

meters	
yards	

8 meters = ? yards

kilograms	
pounds	

15 kilograms = ? pounds

centimeters	
inches	

12 centimeters = ? inches

Using Exponents

Introduction

Program index cards with several expanded form equations such as $8 \times 8 \times 8 =$ and matching exponent form equations such as 8^3. Distribute the cards to students. Have each student walk around the room to find a partner with a matching equation.

Creating the Notebook Page

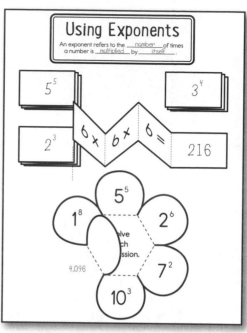

Guide students through the following steps to complete the right-hand page in their notebooks.

1. Add a Table of Contents entry for the Using Exponents pages.

2. Cut out the title and glue it to the top of the page.

3. Complete the explanation. (An exponent refers to the **number** of times a number is **multiplied** by **itself**.)

4. Cut out the four accordion folds. Alternate folds on the dashed lines so that the text is folded inside. Apply glue to the back of the right section of each piece. Attach them to the page in a 2 by 2 arrangement below the title.

5. Write the expression using exponents on top of each accordion fold. Then, find the product of the exponent expression and write it on the blank back of each accordion fold piece.

6. Cut out the six-flap petal fold. Apply glue to the back of the center section and attach it to the bottom of the page.

7. Find the answer for each exponent expression and write it under the petal.

Reflect on Learning

To complete the left-hand page, have each student write an exponent expression of their own choosing. They should show how to solve it using repeated multiplication and find the product. Then, they should explain why using exponents in math is important.

Answer Key
Clockwise from top: 3,125; 64; 49; 1,000; 4,096; 1

Using Exponents

An exponent refers to the _____ of times
a number is _____ by _____.

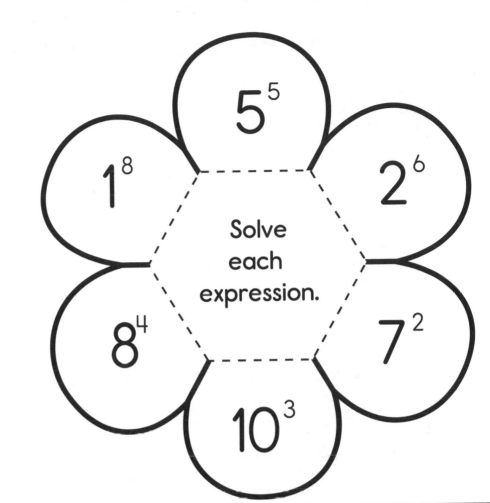

1^8

5^5

2^6

8^4

7^2

10^3

Solve each expression.

6 x	6 x	6 =	
2 x	2 x	2 =	
3 x	3 x	3 x 3 =	
5 x 5	x 5 x	5 x 5 =	

Parts of an Expression

Introduction

Review the parts of expressions by writing simple expressions such as *5 + 3 = 8* and *2 × 6 = 12* on index cards. On the back of the index card, have students rewrite the expression using only the names of the parts of the expression. (For example, *factor times factor equals product.*)

Creating the Notebook Page

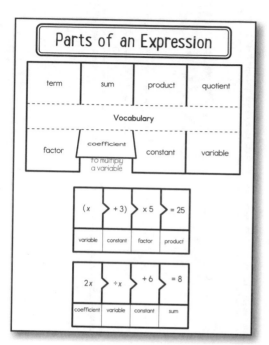

Guide students through the following steps to complete the right-hand page in their notebooks.

1. Add a Table of Contents entry for the Parts of an Expression pages.

2. Cut out the title and glue it to the top of the page.

3. Cut out the flap book. Cut on the solid lines to create eight flaps. Apply glue to the back of the center section and attach it below the title.

4. Write the definition of each word under the flap.

5. Cut out the labeled rectangles and glue them to the bottom of the page, one below the other. Leave space above each one to place the puzzle pieces.

6. Cut out the puzzle pieces and arrange them over the labeled rectangles so that the terms on the pieces match the vocabulary used on the rectangles and so that the expressions make sense. Glue them over the labels they match.

Reflect on Learning

To complete the left-hand page, have students write expressions that result in quotients. Students should label the parts of the expressions with the appropriate vocabulary.

Answer Key
$(x + 3) \times 5 = 25$; $2x \div x + 6 = 8$

Parts of an Expression

term	sum	product	quotient

Vocabulary

factor	coefficient	constant	variable

product
factor
constant
variable

sum
constant
variable
coefficient

(x

2x

+ 6

= 25

+ 3)

÷ x

= 8

x 5

Writing Expressions

Introduction

Draw a table on the board with four columns. Use one of the four mathematical operations as a header for each of the columns. Review using key words to solve word problems by having students brainstorm a list of the key words to look for in word problems. Have students list the words under the appropriate columns and discuss.

Writing Expressions

An __expression__ is a __number__ phrase without an __equal__ sign.

Clue Words				
+	−	⋈ product times multiplied by	÷	variable

a number reduced by 7	$n - 7$
3 times a number divided by 2	$3n \div 2$
$\frac{2}{5}$ of the sum of a number and 8	$\frac{2}{5}(n + 8)$
4 ns taken away from 100	$100 - 4n$
a number subtracted from the product of 8 and 6	$(8 \times 6) - n$
the difference between 20 and a number	$20 - n$

Creating the Notebook Page

Guide students through the following steps to complete the right-hand page in their notebooks.

1. Add a Table of Contents entry for Writing Expressions pages.

2. Cut out the title and glue it to the top of the page.

3. Complete the definition of expression. (An **expression** is a **number** phrase without an **equal** sign.)

4. Cut out the *Clue Words* flap book. Cut on the solid lines to create five flaps. Apply glue to the back of the top section and attach it to the page below the title.

5. Under each flap, write clue words that tell which operation or variable should be used when writing an expression. (Examples: +: increased, added, sum; −: decreased, subtract, minus, take away; ×: product, times; ÷: fractions, divided; variable: "a number," any letter used alone)

6. Cut out the large flap book. Cut on the solid lines to create six flaps. Apply glue to the back of the left section and attach it to the bottom of the page.

7. On the flap, highlight the key words in each practice problem. Write appropriate expressions for each statement. Under each flap, explain how the key word helped you to write the proper expression.

Reflect on Learning

To complete the left-hand page, write the following word problem on the board or provide a copy for students to glue in their notebooks: *Tom made an 85 on his English test, which was 37 points less than twice the grade on his science test.* Have students create an expression to show how to find Tom's score on his science test. Then, describe how writing expressions can be helpful when solving word problems.

Answer Key

From top to bottom: $n - 7$; $3n \div 2$; $\frac{2}{5}(n + 8)$; $100 - 4n$; $(8 \times 6) - n$; 6. $20 - n$

Writing Expressions

An _____ is a _____ phrase without an _____ sign.

Clue Words

+	−	×	÷	variable

a number reduced by 7	
3 times a number divided by 2	
$\frac{2}{5}$ of the sum of a number and 8	
4 *n*s taken away from 100	
a number subtracted from the product of 8 and 6	
the difference between 20 and a number	

Equivalent Expressions

Introduction

Review the distributive property by writing $2x + 4y$ on the board. Have students work with partners to determine what constant can be factored out of the expression.

Creating the Notebook Page

Guide students through the following steps to complete the right-hand page in their notebooks.

1. Add a Table of Contents entry for the Equivalent Expressions pages.

2. Cut out the title and glue it to the top of the page.

3. Cut out the *Strategies* flap book. Apply glue to the back of the center section and attach it below the title.

4. Cut out the two example squares. Glue each one under the strategy it demonstrates.

5. Cut out the rectangle with the two-column chart. Glue it to the middle of the page.

6. Cut out the six expressions. Discuss how to use the strategies to determine if two expressions are equivalent. Glue the expressions under the correct headings.

7. Cut out the *Find the equivalent.* flap book. Cut on the solid lines to create four flaps. Apply glue to the back of the left section and attach it to the bottom of the page.

8. Using the strategies from above, complete each equivalent expression. Under the flap, write the strategy you used.

Equivalent Expressions

Combine variables and constants when possible.	Use the distributive property to extract constants when possible.

Strategies

Equivalent	Not Equivalent
$3(x+4) = 3x+12$	$3(x+4) = 3x+7$
$x+x = 2x$	$x+x = 2+7$
$4x-y = 2x+2x-y$	$4x-y = 4(x-y)$

Find the equivalent.

$2a + 4b$	$=$	___ b)
$b+ b + 2b$	$=$	$\underline{4}\,b$ Combine variables
$3y - y + 8$	$=$	$\underline{2}\,y + \underline{8}$
$5x + 5y + 5$	$=$	$\underline{5}\,(\underline{x} + \underline{y} + \underline{1})$

Reflect on Learning

To complete the left-hand page, have students explain how using equivalent expressions can be helpful when they have to solve problems. Students should give examples to support their explanations.

Answer Key
Equivalent: $x + x = 2x$; $4x - y = 2x + 2x - y$; $3(x + 4) = 3x + 12$; Not Equivalent: $x + x = 2 + x$; $4x - y = 4(x - y)$; $3(x + 4) = 3x + 7$;
Find the Equivalent: **2**(a + **2**b); **4**b; **2**y + 8; **5**(**x** + **y** + **1**)

Equivalent Expressions

Strategies

Combine variables and constants when possible.

Use the distributive property to extract constants when possible.

Equivalent	Not Equivalent

Top right boxes:

$y + 2 - 3 = y - 1$

$y + y = 2y$

$3a + 9b = 3(a) + 3b$

$4(x + y) = 4y + 4x$

Right side boxes:

$x + x = 2x$

$4x - y = 4(x - y)$

$3(x + 4) = 3x + 12$

$3(x + 4) = 3x + 7$

$x + x = 2 + 7$

$4x - y = 2x + 2x - y$

Find the equivalent.

$2a + 4b$	$= \underline{}(a + \underline{}b)$
$b + b + 2b$	$= \underline{}b$
$3y - y + 8$	$= \underline{}y + \underline{}$
$5x + 5y + 5$	$= \underline{}(\underline{} + \underline{} + \underline{})$

Evaluating Expressions

Introduction

Review the parts of an expression by writing *x + 3y* on the board. Have students label each part with the correct vocabulary. Emphasize the definition of a variable. Have students evaluate the expression *2 + 3 x 4.* Demonstrate how both expressions are the same, but one has used values to replace the variables.

Creating the Notebook Page

Guide students through the following steps to complete the right-hand page in their notebooks.

1. Add a Table of Contents entry for the Evaluating Expressions pages.

2. Cut out the title and glue it to the top of the page.

3. Complete the sentence below the title. (An **expression** can be **evaluated** by **substituting values** for the **variables**.)

4. Cut out the flap book with Steps 1 to 3. Cut on the solid lines to create three flaps. Apply glue to the back of the left section and attach it below the title.

5. Under each flap, write a description of the step for evaluating an expression. (1. Rewrite the expression, leaving blanks for the variables. 2. Substitute the given values for the variables. 3. Use order of operations to evaluate the expression.)

6. Solve the example problem. If desired, color code the flaps and each step of the process to match.

7. Cut out the *Evaluate each* flap book. Apply glue to the back of the center section and attach it the bottom of the page.

8. Under each flap, evaluate the expression using the values given.

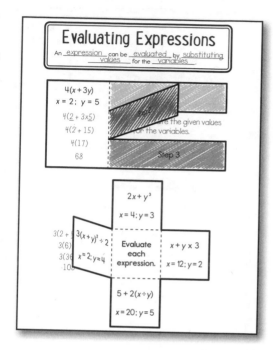

Reflect on Learning

To complete the left-hand page, have students create a two-variable expression. Have students solve the expression using three different sets of values for the variables. Students should explain why the expression yields a different result when different values are used for the variables.

Answer Key
Clockwise from top: 35; 42; 28; 54

Evaluating Expressions

An _____ can be _____ by _____ for the _____.

$4(x + 3y)$	Step 1
$x = 2$; $y = 5$	Step 2
	Step 3

$2x + y^3$

$x = 4$; $y = 3$

| $3(x + y)^2 \div 2$ | Evaluate each expression. | $x + y \times 3$ |
| $x = 2$; $y = 4$ | | $x = 12$; $y = 2$ |

$5 + 2(x \div y)$

$x = 20$; $y = 5$

Solving One-Variable Addition and Subtraction Equations

Introduction

Write $b = 3 + 4 - 2$ on the board. Have students find the value of b. Explain that even when there are constants on both sides of the equation, similar steps can be used to solve the problem.

Creating the Notebook Page

Guide students through the following steps to complete the right-hand page in their notebooks.

1. Add a Table of Contents entry for the Solving One-Variable Addition and Subtraction Equations pages.

2. Cut out the title and glue it to the top of the page.

3. Cut out the *Solving Equations* piece and glue it to the left side of the top of the page.

4. Solve the example problem. If desired, color code the flaps and each step of the process to match.

5. Cut out the *Equation* flaps. Apply glue to the back of the left section of each flap. Attach them to the right side of the page.

6. Cut out the numbered pieces and glue each one under the *Equation* flaps so that they are hidden.

7. Use the steps from the *Solving Equations* piece to show the work as each equation is solved.

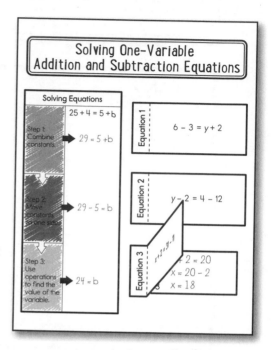

Reflect on Learning

To complete the left-hand page, have students think of a situation in which they would use an addition or subtraction equation to solve a problem. Have students show how they would solve the equation.

Answer Key
Equation 1: $3 = y + 2$; $3 - 2 = y$; $1 = y$; Equation 2: $y - 2 = 8$; $y = -8 + 2$; $y = -6$; Equation 3: $x + 2 = 20$;
$x = 20 - 2$; $x = 18$

Solving One-Variable
Addition and Subtraction Equations

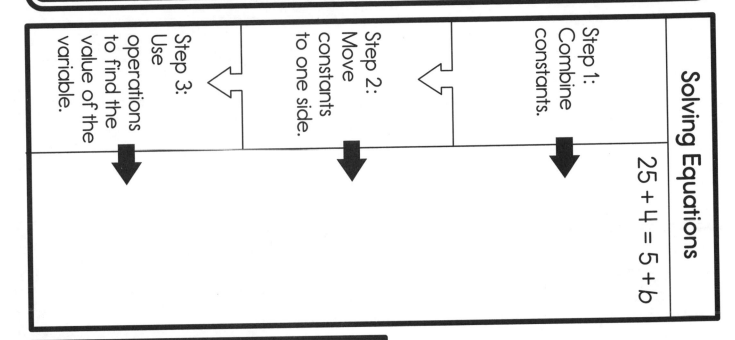

Solving Equations	$25 + 4 = 5 + b$
Step 1: Combine constants.	
Step 2: Move constants to one side.	
Step 3: Use operations to find the value of the variable.	

Equation 1	$6 - 3 = y + 2$
Equation 2	$y - 2 = 4 - 12$
Equation 3	$x + 2 = 31 - 11$

1
2
3

1
2
3

1
2
3

Solving One-Variable Multiplication and Division Equations

Each student will need a brass paper fastener to complete this page.

Introduction

Write *2 + x = 6* on the board. Have students find the value of *x* and explain how they used inverse operations to solve the expression. Ask students to hypothesize how they might solve expressions that use multiplication or division instead of addition or subtraction.

Creating the Notebook Page

Guide students through the following steps to complete the right-hand page in their notebooks.

1. Add a Table of Contents entry for the Solving One-Variable Multiplication and Division Equations pages.

2. Cut out the title and glue it to the top of the page.

3. Cut out the accordion fold. Starting with the arrow end, fold the piece back and forth on the dashed lines to create an accordion fold with the arrow on top. Apply glue to the back of the last flap. Attach it to the top left side of the page.

4. Cut out the rectangle and glue it to the top right of the page. Solve the example problem. If desired, color code the steps on the accordion fold and each step of the process to match.

5. Cut out the circles and place the smaller circle on top. Push a brass paper fastener through the center dots of the circles to attach them. It may be helpful to create a hole in each piece separately first. Apply glue to the back of the large circle. Attach it to the bottom of the page with *3x + 2* and *3x + 7* at the top. Do not press the brass paper fastener through the page.

6. Spin the smaller circle to create a variety of equations. Write the equations around the outside of the circle. Then, solve for the variable.

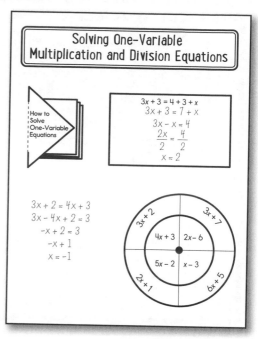

Reflect on Learning

To complete the left-hand page, have each student think of an expression that involves multiplication or division with a variable *x*. Assign partners and have them place their expressions on opposite sides of an equation and then solve for the variable.

Solving One-Variable Multiplication and Division Equations

Step 1: Combine constants.

Step 2: Move constants to one side and variables to the other.

Step 3: Use operations to reduce the equation.

Step 4: Multiply or divide to find the value of the variable.

How to Solve One-Variable Equations

$3x + 3 = 4 + 3 + x$

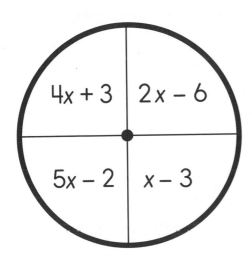

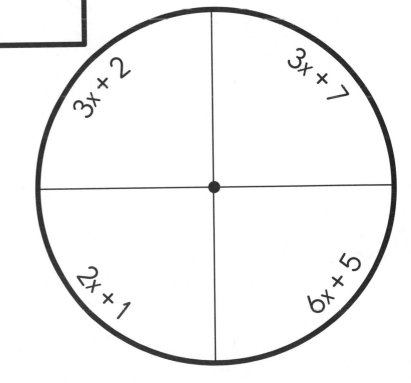

Graphing Inequalities

Introduction

Write *4 < 6* on the board. Draw a number line and use it to demonstrate that this statement is true. Have students work with partners to name two more true statements that can be proven with the number line. Then, ask students to consider how they would compare a variable to a known value. For example, *The price of the notebook was less than $5.00.*

Creating the Notebook Page

Guide students through the following steps to complete the right-hand page in their notebooks.

1. Add a Table of Contents entry for the Graphing Inequalities pages.

2. Cut out the title and glue it to the top of the page.

3. Cut out the T-chart and attach it to the top left of the page.

4. Complete the chart by writing the symbols that are represented with open or closed circles on the correct side of the chart.

5. Cut out the *Example Inequalities* and blank number line flap books. Cut on the solid lines to create six flaps on each book. Apply glue to the gray glue area on the blank number lines flap book and place the *Example Inequalities* flap on top to create a stacked flap book. Apply glue to the back of the left side of the flap book and attach it to the top right of the page.

6. Write the appropriate symbol on top of each flap. Then, create an example inequality on the back of the flap. Graph the inequality on the number line flap. Under the number line flap, describe why you chose that circle type and direction when graphing.

7. Cut out the *Write Inequalities* flap book. Cut on the solid lines to create five flaps. Apply glue to the back of the left section and attach it to the bottom of the page.

8. Write the inequality that is represented by each number line under the flap.

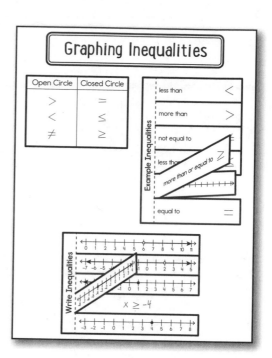

Reflect on Learning

To complete the left-hand page, have students create one inequality statement related to speed limits and another related to text messaging plans. Then, students should draw number lines to represent both inequalities graphically.

Answer Key
From top to bottom: $x > 6$; $x \neq 2$; $x \leq 1$; $x \geq -4$; $x = 4$

Graphing Inequalities

	Open Circle
	Closed Circle

Write Inequalities

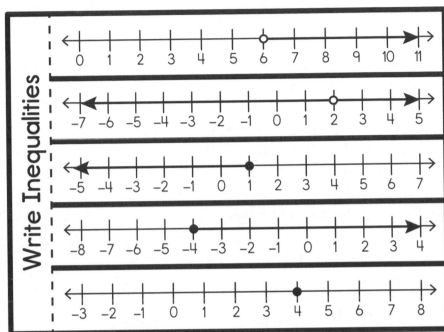

Example Inequalities

less than	
more than	
not equal to	
less than or equal to	
more than or equal to	
equal to	

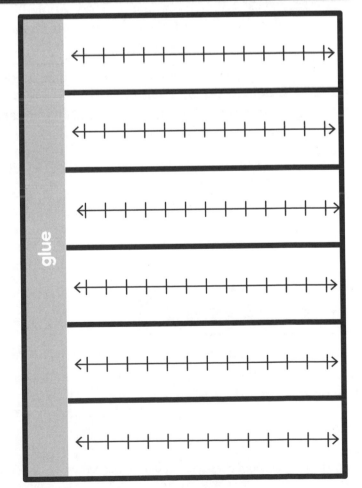

glue

Dependent and Independent Variables

Introduction

Present students with the following situation: *If you exercise for a set amount of time, you will burn a particular number of calories.* Ask students to identify the two variables in this situation (time and calories). Then, ask students to identify the cause and effect relationship between the variables (cause = time, effect = calories burned).

Creating the Notebook Page

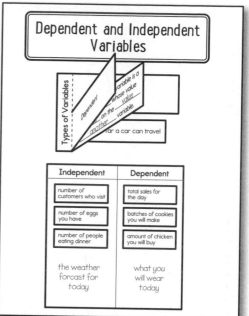

Guide students through the following steps to complete the right-hand page in their notebooks.

1. Add a Table of Contents entry for the Dependent and Independent Variables pages.

2. Cut out the title and glue it to the top of the page.

3. Cut out the two flap books. Cut on the solid lines to create two flaps on each piece. Apply glue to the gray glue section and place the *Type of Variable* flap book directly on top. Then, apply glue to the back of the left section and attach the flap book below the title.

4. Complete the definitions on the flaps under each type of variable. (Independent: An **independent** variable is a **variable** whose value **causes** another **variable** to **change**. Dependent: A **dependent** variable is a **variable** whose value **depends** on the **value** of **another** variable.)

5. Cut out the *amount of gas* and *how far* pieces. Glue them under the bottom flap of the correct variable type.

6. Cut out the T-chart. Glue it to the bottom of the page.

7. Cut out the three rectangle pairs. Cut out each pair and glue the pieces to the correct sides of the T-chart. Think of at least one additional example of a variable pair and add it to the chart.

Reflect on Learning

To complete the left-hand page, have students think of a science experiment to conduct using independent and dependent variables. Students should explain their experiment in terms of the dependent and independent variables. Then, have students describe several values they would test in their experiment for the independent variable.

Answer Key
Independent: number of people eating dinner, number of eggs you have, number of customers who visit; Dependent: amount of chicken you will buy; batches of cookies you will make; total sales for the day

Dependent and Independent Variables

Types of Variables

Independent

Dependent

An _____ variable is a _____ whose value _____ to _____.

A _____ variable is a _____ whose value _____ on the _____ variable.

glue

| how far a car can travel | amount of gas in a car |

Independent	Dependent

total sales for the day

number of customers who visit

batches of cookies you will make

number of eggs you have

number of people eating dinner

amount of chicken you will buy

Areas of Polygons

© Carson-Dellosa • CD-104910

Introduction

Draw a $3 \times n$ rectangle on the board. Remind students that when you find area, you are finding how many square units it will take to cover the area. Tell students that the area of the rectangle given is 12. Have students talk with partners to find the missing side of the rectangle. Then, draw several more rectangles on the board with one side length and the total area given. Work with students to find the missing dimensions.

Creating the Notebook Page

Guide students through the following steps to complete the right-hand page in their notebooks.

1. Add a Table of Contents entry for the Areas of Polygons pages.

2. Cut out the title and glue it to the top of the page.

3. Cut out the variables piece and glue it below the title.

4. Cut out the *Triangles* flap book and the matching explanation flap book. Cut on the solid line to create two flaps on each book. Apply glue to the gray glue section and place the *Triangles* flap book on top to create a stacked flap book. Apply glue to the back of the top section and attach it below the variables piece.

5. Read through the information under each type of triangle. Then, use the formula on the flap to complete the sample problem under the flap.

6. Cut out the *Other Polygons* flap book and the matching explanation flap book. Cut on the solid lines to create four flaps on each book. Apply glue to the gray glue section at the top of the explanations piece, and place the *Other Polygons* piece on top to create a stacked flap book. Apply glue to the back of the top section and attach it to the bottom of the page.

7. Read through the information under each type of polygon. Then, use the formula on the flap to complete the sample problem under each flap.

Reflect on Learning

To complete the left-hand page, ask students to list an example of a time when they would need to find the area of each of the example polygons.

Answer Key

Right Triangles: $\frac{1}{2}(4 \times 5) = 10$ sq. units; Other Triangles: $\frac{1}{2}(6 \times 6) + \frac{1}{2}(6 \times 3) = 27$ sq. units; Rectangles: $5 \times 3 = 15$ sq. units; Parallelograms: $10 \times 6 = 60$ sq. units; Trapezoids: $\frac{6+8}{2} = $ sq. units ; Irregular shapes: $(8 \times 4) + (3 \times 4) = 44$ sq. units

Areas of Polygons

b = base, h = height

l = length, and w = width

Triangles

Right Triangles

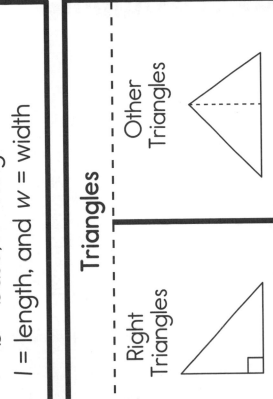

Other Triangles

Formula:
$\frac{1}{2}(b \times h)$

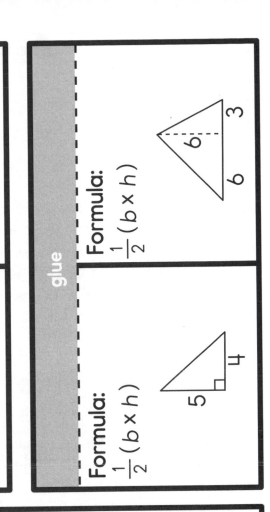

5

4

Formula:
$\frac{1}{2}(b \times h)$

6

6

3

Other Polygons

| Rectangles | Parallelograms | Trapezoids | Irregular Shapes |

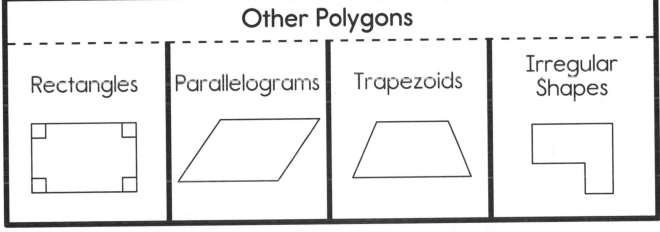

Formula:

$l \times w$

5

3

Formula:

$b \times h$

6

10

Formula:

$\dfrac{b_1 + b_2}{2} \times h$

6

4

8

Break the shape into regular polygons. Then find the areas and add.

8

4

5

4

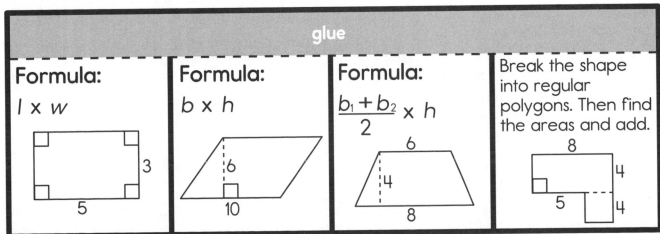

Graphing Polygons

Introduction

Draw a coordinate grid on the board. Draw a rectangle and a right triangle on the coordinate grid. Discuss the characteristics of rectangles and right triangles by showing how the vertices of each polygon are placed on the grid.

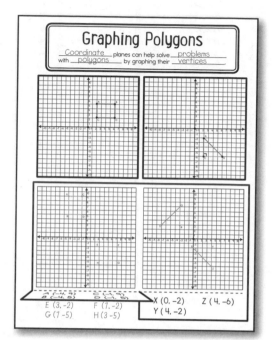

Creating the Notebook Page

Guide students through the following steps to complete the right-hand page in their notebooks.

1. Add a Table of Contents entry for the Graphing Polygons pages.

2. Cut out the title and glue it to the top of the page.

3. Complete the explanation under the title. (**Coordinate** planes can help solve **problems** with **polygons** by graphing their **vertices**.)

4. Cut out the two coordinate grids and glue them to the top of the page.

5. Trace the polygons on the squares in the coordinate planes using a different color for each shape.

6. Cut out the large flap book. Cut on the solid line to create two flaps. Apply glue to the back of the top section and attach it to the bottom of the page.

7. Using the same colors as used in step 5, draw the shapes indicated on the flap.

8. Discuss how to use the given information and the dimensions of each shape in order to create congruent figures. Draw another of each shape on the plane and record the points of the vertices under the correct flap.

Reflect on Learning

To complete the left-hand page, have students draw a coordinate grid and graph another type of polygon on the grid. Students should explain how to find the coordinates of the vertices when you create a polygon on a coordinate grid.

Graphing Polygons

_____ planes can help solve _____
with _____ by graphing their _____.

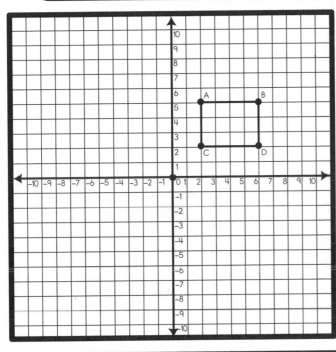

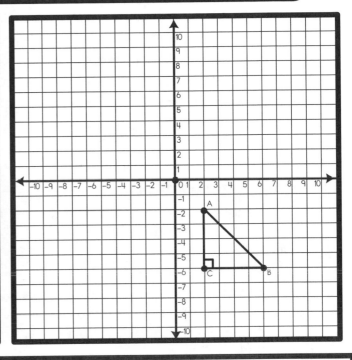

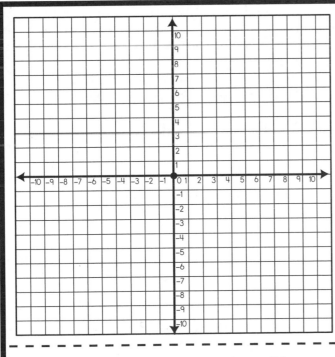

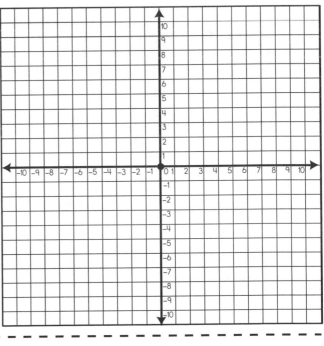

A (–4, 9)	C (–1, 9)	X (0, –2)	Z (4, –6)
B (–4, 5)	D (–1, 5)	Y (4, –2)	

Volume of Rectangular Solids

Distribute a handful of base ten unit cubes to each pair of students. Have students use the unit cubes to make a model cube that is two cubes high, two cubes wide, and two cubes tall. Partners should work together to determine how many of the smaller cubes they used to create the large cube. Explain that the total number of unit cubes used determines the volume of the cube.

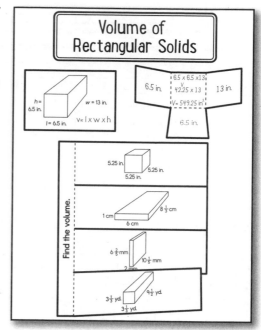

Creating the Notebook Page

Guide students through the following steps to complete the right-hand page in their notebooks.

1. Add a Table of Contents entry for the Volume of Rectangular Solids pages.

2. Cut out the title and glue it to the top of the page.

4. Cut out the piece showing a rectangular solid and glue it to the top left of the page. Write the formula for volume on the lower right corner of the piece ($V = l \times w \times h$).

5. Cut out the three-flap flap book. Apply glue to the gray glue section and attach it to the top right of the page. Fold the flaps in so that the word *length* appears on top.

6. Record the length, height, and width of the example solid on the back of the appropriate flaps. Then, multiply the dimensions together and write the volume on the blank center square (549.25 in.²).

7. Cut out the flap book. Cut on the solid lines to create four flaps. Apply glue to the back of the left section and attach it to the bottom of the page.

8. Use the formula to find the volume of the solids on the flaps and record the answers under the flaps.

Reflect on Learning

To complete the left-hand page, have students choose one of the models from the bottom of the right-hand page. Students should explain how increasing or decreasing the measure of one of the sides would affect the total volume.

Answer Key

From top to bottom: 144.70 in.³; 50 cm³; $130 \frac{14}{25}$ mm³; $105 \frac{5}{9}$ yd.³

Volume of Rectangular Solids

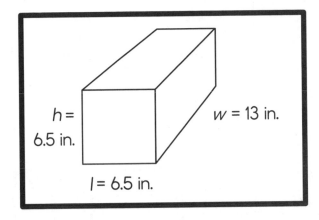

$h = 6.5$ in.
$w = 13$ in.
$l = 6.5$ in.

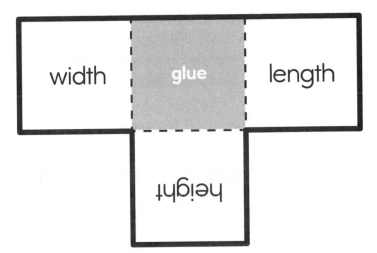

width   glue   length

height

Find the volume.

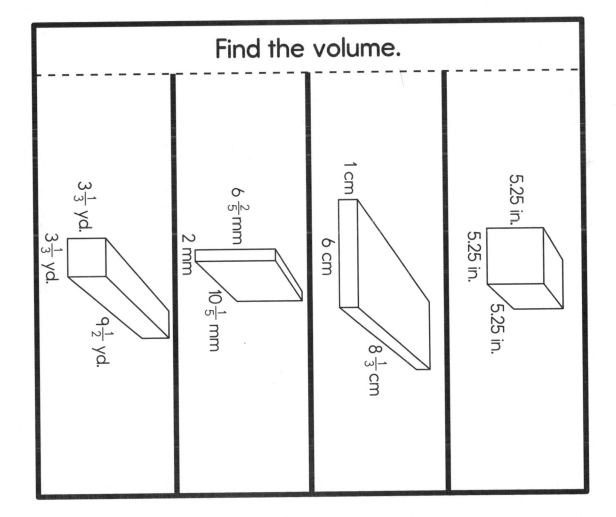

$3\frac{1}{3}$ yd.

$3\frac{1}{3}$ yd.

$9\frac{1}{2}$ yd.

$6\frac{2}{5}$ mm

2 mm

$10\frac{1}{5}$ mm

1 cm

6 cm

$8\frac{1}{3}$ cm

5.25 in.

5.25 in.

5.25 in.

Surface Area

Introduction

Draw a cube on the board that is 8 in. × 8 in. × 8 in. Have students deconstruct the cube by naming the number of faces and edges. Then, have students find the area of one of the faces.

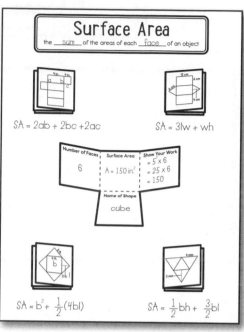

Creating the Notebook Page

Guide students through the following steps to complete the right-hand page in their notebooks.

1. Add a Table of Contents entry for the Surface Area pages.

2. Cut out the title and glue it to the top of the page.

3. Complete the definition (the **sum** of the areas of each **face** of the object).

4. Cut out each of the four-square flaps. Fold each of the tabs in on the dashed lines so that a blank square appears on the top. Apply glue to the back of the *Surface Area* square on each piece and arrange them on the page.

5. Cut out the small squares with the nets. Glue each one to one of the blank squares.

6. Unfold each square and enter the appropriate information on each.

7. Below each square, write an equation to represent its surface area. (For example, SA = 2*ab* + 2*bc* + 2*ac*.)

Reflect on Learning

To complete the left-hand page, have students consider when they might need to use the surface area of a figure in real life. Students should describe at least two real-life situations. Then, students should write an equation to find the surface area for each.

Answer Key
Name: Cube; Faces: 6; Surface Area: 150 in.²; Name: Triangular Prism; Faces: 5; Surface Area: 240 cm²; Name: Square Pyramid; Faces: 5; Surface Area: 28 ft.²; Name: Triangular Pyramid; Faces: 4; Surface Area: 48 mm²; Name: Rectangular Prism; Faces: 6; Surface Area: 176 in.²

Surface Area

the _____ of the areas of each _____ of an object

Show Your Work	Number of Faces	Surface Area	Show Your Work
Surface Area	Name of Shape	Name of Shape	Number of Faces
Number of Faces	Name of Shape	Name of Shape	Surface Area
Show Your Work	Surface Area	Number of Faces	Show Your Work
Number of Faces	Surface Area	Show Your Work
Name of Shape

Statistical Questions

Introduction

Write this question on the board: *What time did you wake up this morning?* Collect responses from students and tally responses on the board. Point out that this data represents a set of statistics about the class. The question that was asked has many possible answers and is considered a statistical question.

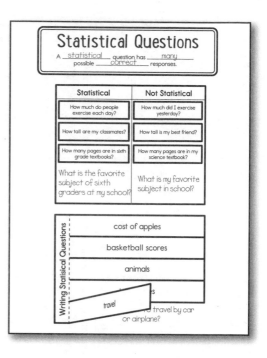

Creating the Notebook Page

Guide students through the following steps to complete the right-hand page in their notebooks.

1. Add a Table of Contents entry for the Statistical Questions pages.

2. Cut out the title and glue it to the top of the page.

3. Complete the explanation below the title. (A **statistical** question has **many** possible **correct** responses.)

4. Cut out the T-chart piece and glue it below the title.

5. Discuss the differences between statistical questions and questions that are not statistical.

6. Cut out the six question pieces. Glue the questions to the correct columns of the T-chart. Think of at least one additional example of each type of question and write it in the chart.

7. Cut out the flap book. Cut on the solid lines to create five flaps. Apply glue to the back of the left section and attach it to the bottom of the page.

8. Write a statistical question about each category described under the flap.

Reflect on Learning

To complete the left-hand page, have students write three more statistical questions and list some of the possible responses for each question. Students should explain why each of their questions are statistical.

Answer Key
Statistical: How tall are my classmates? How much do people exercise each day? How many pages are in sixth grade textbooks? Not Statistical: How many pages are in my science textbook? How tall is my best friend? How much did I exercise yesterday?

Statistical Questions

A _____ question has _____ possible _____ responses.

Statistical	Not Statistical

How tall are my classmates?

How much do people exercise each day?

How tall is my best friend?

How much did I exercise yesterday?

How many pages are in sixth grade textbooks?

How many pages are in my science textbook?

Writing Statistical Questions

cost of apples

basketball scores

animals

test scores

travel

Measures of Center

Each student will need a brass paper fastener to complete this page.

Introduction

Write the following data set on the board: *2, 4, 5, 5, 7, 8, 9.* Explain that there are many ways to describe the data set. Guide students to describe the data using mean (or average), median, and mode. Explain that describing data in this way uses measures of center. These descriptions are ways of telling what comes in the middle of a data set.

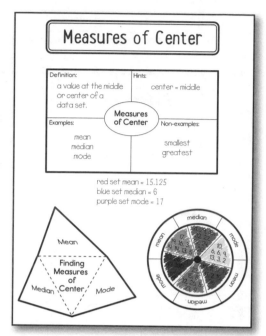

Creating the Notebook Page

Guide students through the following steps to complete the right-hand page in their notebooks.

1. Add a Table of Contents entry for the Measures of Center pages.

2. Cut out the title and glue it to the top of the page.

3. Cut out the Frayer Model and glue it below the title. Complete the Frayer Model.

4. Cut out the *Finding Measures* flap book. Fold the triangle flaps in on the dashed lines. Apply glue to the back of the flap book and attach it to the bottom left of the page. Write directions for finding each measure of center under the appropriate flap.

5. Cut out the circles. Color each section of the smaller circle a different shade and place it on top. Push a brass paper fastener through the center dots to attach them. It may be helpful to create a hole in each piece separately first. Apply glue to the back of the large circle. Attach it to the bottom of the page. Do not press the brass paper fastener through the page.

6. Spin the top circle so each data set matches up with a measure of center. Then, work around the circle to find the designated measure of center for the matching data set. Use the color coding to record the answers of each set of data, which measure of center is found, and the results on the page beside the spinner.

Reflect on Learning

To complete the left-hand page, ask students to collect a data set with at least eight values showing how far classmates live from the school. Then, have students find the measures of center for the distances their classmates live from the school.

Answer Key
(Set 31, 29, . . .) mean: 27.5, median: 28, mode: none; (Set 10, 6, . . .) mean: 7, median: 6, mode: 6; (Set 10, 11, . . .) mean: 14, median: 14.5, mode: 17; (Set 23, 15, . . .) mean: 15.125, median: 13.5, mode: 23; (Set 83, 86, . . .) mean: 93, median: 93, mode: 99; (Set 17, 19, . . .) mean: 12.625, median: 14, mode: 14

Measures of Center

Definition:

Hints:

Measures of Center

Examples:

Non-examples:

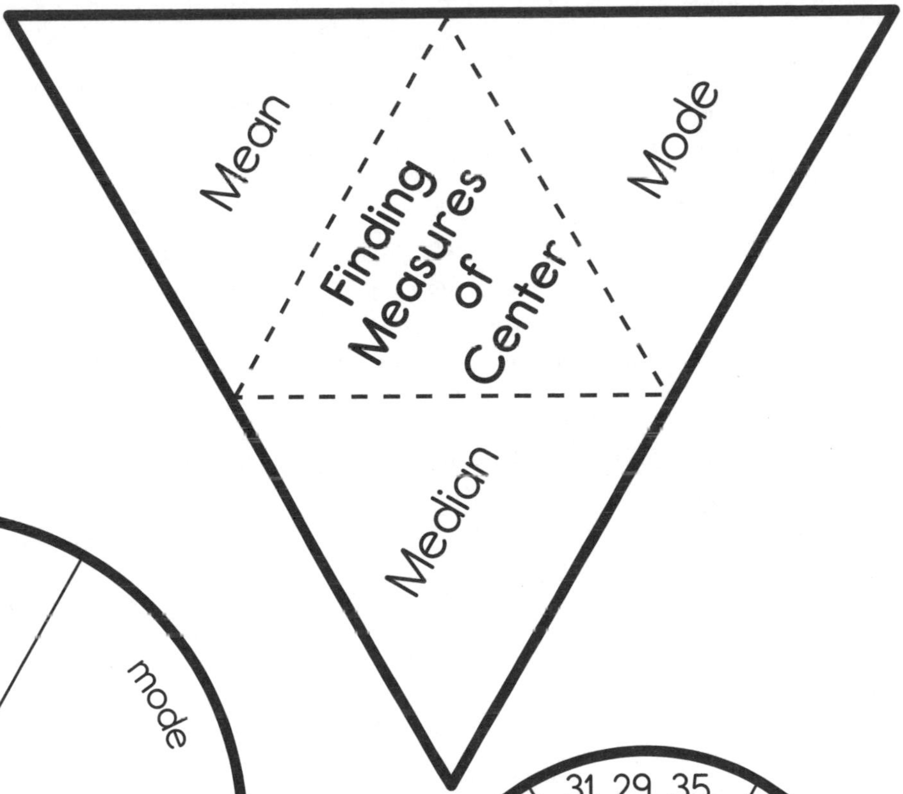

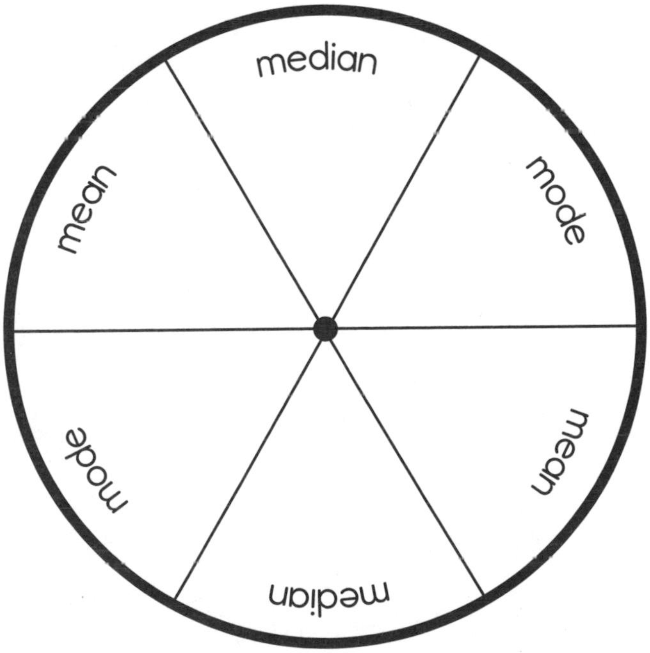

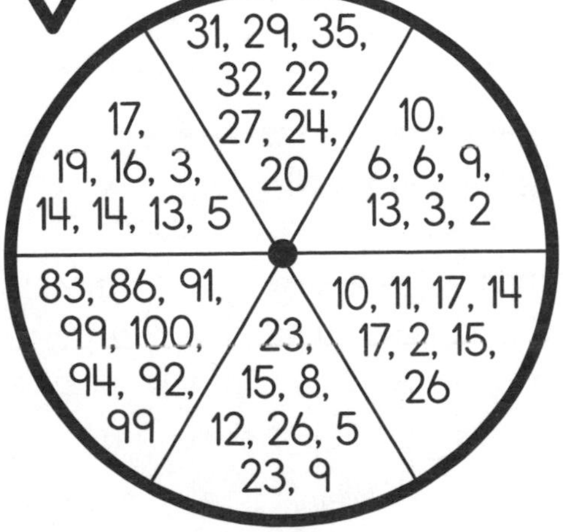

Finding Measures of Center

Mean

Mode

Median

Median

mean

median

mode

mean

mode

median

31, 29, 35, 32, 22, 27, 24, 20

10, 6, 6, 9, 13, 3, 2

17, 19, 16, 3, 14, 14, 13, 5

83, 86, 91, 99, 100, 94, 92, 99

23, 15, 8, 12, 26, 5, 23, 9

10, 11, 17, 14, 17, 2, 15, 26

Measures of Variability

Introduction

Explain that when working with a data set, it is common to describe the data using measures of center, but data can also be described by using the differences between the values. These are called measures of variability. Write the following numbers on the board: *3, 5, 6, 6, 8, 9, 10.* Have students describe the data set using differences between the values.

Creating the Notebook Page

Guide students through the following steps to complete the right-hand page in their notebooks.

1. Add a Table of Contents entry for the Measures of Variability pages.

2. Cut out the title and glue it to the top of the page.

3. Cut out the two rectangular pieces on the solid lines. Fold each piece on the dashed lines so that the print appears on the outside. Apply glue to the gray glue section and place the other folded piece on top so that the folds are nested together and create a book with four cascading flaps. Make sure that the inside pages are facing up so that the edges of both pages are visible. Apply glue to the back of the book and attach it to the top of the page.

4. Add *Range, Interquartile Range* (IQR) and *Mean Absolute Deviation* (MAD) to the tabs of the flip book.

5. Fill in the blanks to complete the explanation of measures of variability. (Measures of **variability** are ways to **measure** the **spread** in a **set** of **data**.)

6. Take notes inside the flip book about how to find each measure of variability.

7. Cut out the data flap and glue it to the bottom of the page.

8. Find each measure of variability for the sets of data given and record them on the table. Show your work under the flap

The following image shows the Measures of Variability notebook page:

Measures of Variability

Measures of __variability__ are ways to __measure__ the __spread__ in a __set__ of __data__.

the smallest number from the largest number.
Range
Interquartile Range
Mean Absolute Deviation

Data	Range	IQR	MAD
11, 3, 4, 7, 8, 4, 5	8	4	2.29
10, 17, 18, 15, 16, 10, 22	12	8	3.22
70, 75, 95, 100, 90	30	25	10.8
37, 33, 36, 37, 33, 41	8	6	2.17
14, 31, 34, 21, 13, 28, 33	21	19	7.59
23, 41, 31, 27, 9, 13	3.2	25	9

Reflect on Learning

To complete the left-hand page, have students find the measures of center and variability for the following data set: 6, 8, 4, 2, 8, 5, 7, 9, 8. Have students explain why measures of center and variability are necessary to get a complete picture of a data set.

Answer Key
From top: 8, 4, 2.29; 12, 8, 3.22; 30, 25, 10.8; 8, 6, 2.17; 21, 19, 7.59; 32, 25, 9

glue

glue

Measures of _____
are ways to _____
the _____ in a _____
_____ of _____.

Data	Range	IQR	MAD
11, 3, 4, 7, 8, 4, 5			
10, 17, 18, 15, 16, 10, 22			
70, 75, 95, 100, 90			
37, 33, 36, 37, 33, 41			
14, 31, 34, 21, 13, 28, 33			
23, 41, 31, 27, 9, 13			

Measures of Variability

Box and Whisker Plots

Introduction

Have students list ways to graph data. Record their ideas on the board. Divide students into small groups based on the number of graphs they have listed. Assign one type of graph to each group. Then, have students work in their small groups to describe what kind of information they can get from their assigned graph type. Allow time for groups to share their information.

Creating the Notebook Page

Guide students through the following steps to complete the right-hand page in their notebooks.

1. Add a Table of Contents entry for the Box and Whisker Plots pages.

2. Cut out the title and glue it to the top of the page.

3. Cut out the flap book. Cut on the solid lines to create five flaps. Apply glue to the back of the top section and attach it to the top of the page.

4. Under each flap, write a description of the step. (1. Find the median of the data set. 2. Find the median of the lower half, the lower quartile. 3. Find the median of the upper half, the upper quartile. 4. Draw a line segment from the low extreme to the high extreme with a cross-segment at the median. 5. Draw a box around the median cross-segment that has its left and right bounds at the lower and upper quartiles.)

5. Create a box and whisker plot using the sample data set shown. If desired, color code the flaps and each step of the process to match.

6. Cut out the *Science Test Scores* piece. Glue it below the step-by-step flap book.

7. Cut out the labels and glue them to the example to label each part of a box-and-whisker plot.

8. At the bottom of the page, describe the data in the example box-and-whisker plot using two to three sentences and the appropriate vocabulary.

Reflect on Learning

To complete the left-hand page, have students create Venn Diagrams explaining how the information they can get from a box-and-whisker plot is similar to and different from other types of graphs.

Box and Whisker Plots

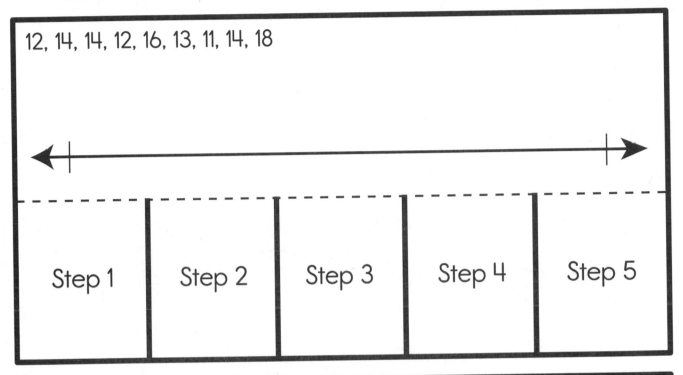

12, 14, 14, 12, 16, 13, 11, 14, 18

| Step 1 | Step 2 | Step 3 | Step 4 | Step 5 |

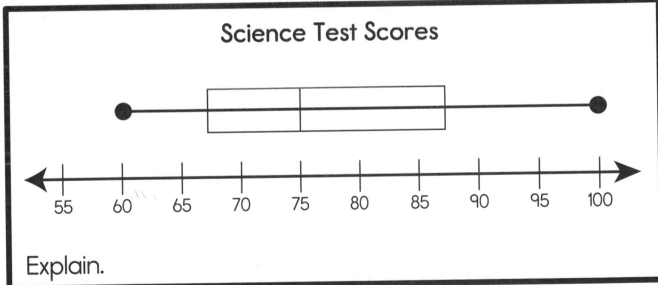

Science Test Scores

Explain.

| median | low extreme | lower quartile | upper quartile |

| high extreme |

Histograms

Introduction

Write the following data set on the board: *65, 70, 70, 75, 80, 85, 85, 85, 90, 90, 95, 100.* Have students talk with partners or a small group to decide how they would graph the data set. Allow time for students to share their selected graphs. Explain that histograms are one way of graphing data by using data ranges and bars of different heights.

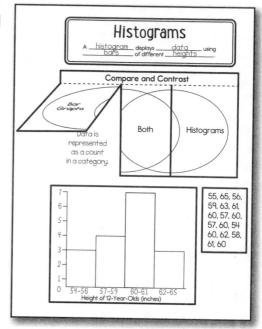

Creating the Notebook Page

Guide students through the following steps to complete the right-hand page in their notebooks.

1. Add a Table of Contents entry for the Histograms pages.

2. Cut out the title and glue it to the top of the page.

3. Complete the explanation below the title. (A **histogram** displays **data** using **bars** of different **heights**.)

4. Cut out the Venn diagram flap book. Cut on the solid lines to create three flaps. Apply glue to the back of the top section and attach it to the top of the page.

5. Under each flap, describe how histograms and bar graphs are similar and different. (Some examples are: Bar Graphs: data is represented as a count in a category; Both: data is represented using bars; Histograms: continuous data is represented in ranges)

6. Cut out the set of data and glue it to the bottom right of the page.

7. Cut out the blank histogram and glue it to the bottom left of the page.

8. Use the data set to create an appropriate histogram.

Reflect on Learning

To complete the left-hand page, have students describe one situation in which they would create a bar graph and another situation in which they would create a histogram to display data. Have students explain why they chose each graph type for the different types of data.

Histograms

A _____ displays _____ using
_____ of different _____.

Compare and Contrast

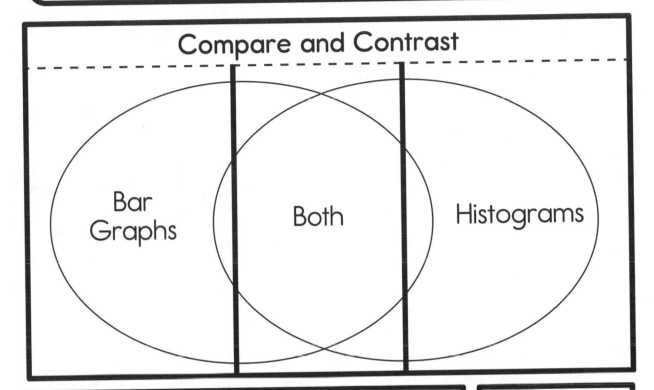

Bar Graphs | Both | Histograms

55, 65, 56, 59, 63, 61, 60, 57, 60, 57, 60, 54, 60, 62, 58, 61, 60

Height of 12-Year-Olds (inches)

Summarizing Data Sets

Introduction

Review the types of data displays by drawing examples on the board. Have students work in small groups to summarize the data displayed on each graph. Allow time for each group to share their summaries with the class.

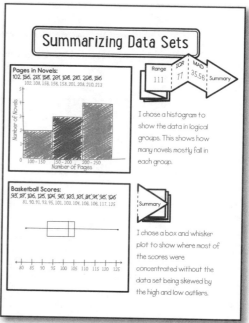

Creating the Notebook Page

Guide students through the following steps to complete the right-hand page in their notebooks.

1. Add a Table of Contents entry for the Summarizing Data Sets pages.

2. Cut out the title and glue it to the top of the page.

3. Cut out one of the data sets and glue it to the top left of the page.

4. Cut out one of the arrow accordion folds. Starting with the arrow end on top, accordion fold on the dashed lines. Apply glue to the back of the last section. Attach it to the top right of the page.

5. Unfold the accordion fold and calculate each measure based on the data set. Then, decide on the best data display and create it in the space below the data set. Finally, explain the data set and your graph choice on the back of the accordion fold.

6. Repeat steps 3–6 with the remaining pieces on the bottom half of the page.

Reflect on Learning

To complete the left-hand page, have students create surveys or research questions that can be answered with data collection. After collecting data, have students summarize and graph their data appropriately and then explain why the data they collected is appropriate for their summaries and graphs.

Answer Key
Basketball Scores: mode: 106; median: 102; mean: 101; range: 44; IQR: 15; MAD: 9.17; Pages in Novels: mode: 156; median: 158; mean: 168; range: 111; IQR: 77; MAD: 35.56

Summarizing Data Sets

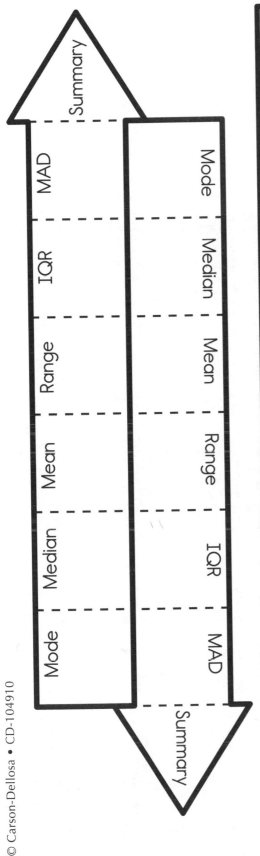

Basketball Scores:
93, 117, 106, 125, 104, 90, 103, 101, 81, 91, 95, 106

Pages in Novels:
102, 156, 213, 158, 201, 108, 210, 208, 156

Tabs

Cut out each tab and label it. Apply glue to the back of each tab and align it on the outside edge of the page with only the label section showing beyond the edge. Then, fold each tab to seal the page inside.

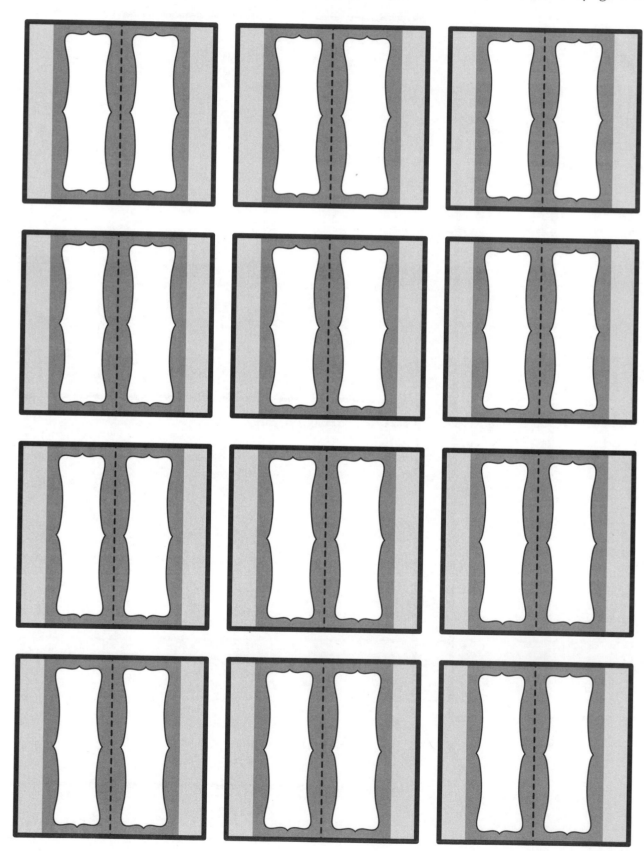

Cut out the KWL chart and cut on the solid lines to create three separate flaps. Apply glue to the back of the Topic section to attach the chart to a notebook page.

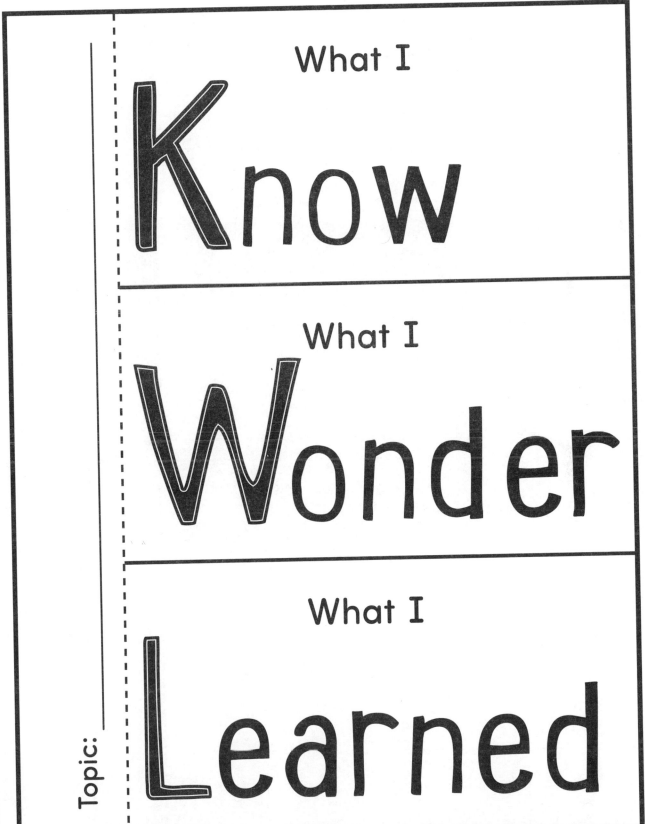

Topic:

What I

Know

What I

Wonder

What I

Learned

Library Pocket

Cut out the library pocket on the solid lines. Fold in the side tabs and apply glue to them before folding up the front of the pocket. Apply glue to the back of the pocket to attach it to a notebook page.

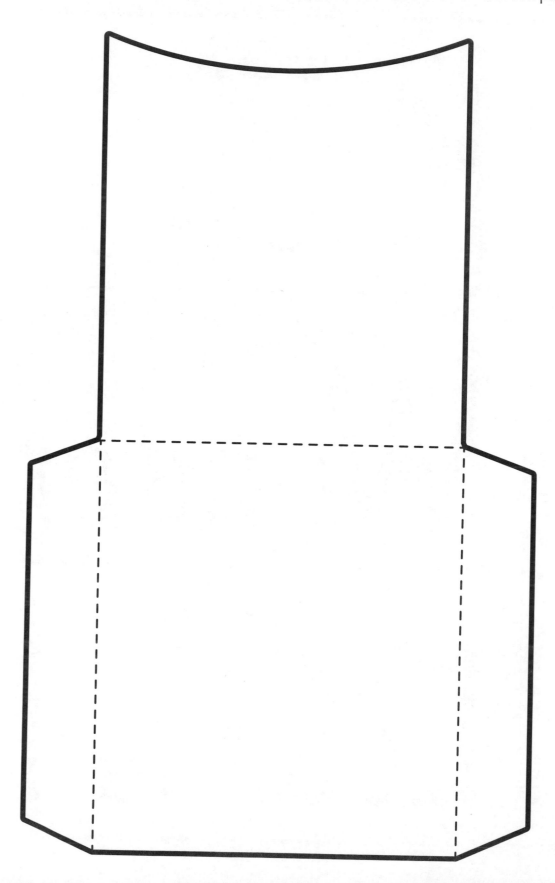

80

Envelope

Cut out the envelope on the solid lines. Fold in the side tabs and apply glue to them before folding up the rectangular front of the envelope. Fold down the triangular flap to close the envelope. Apply glue to the back of the envelope to attach it to a notebook page.

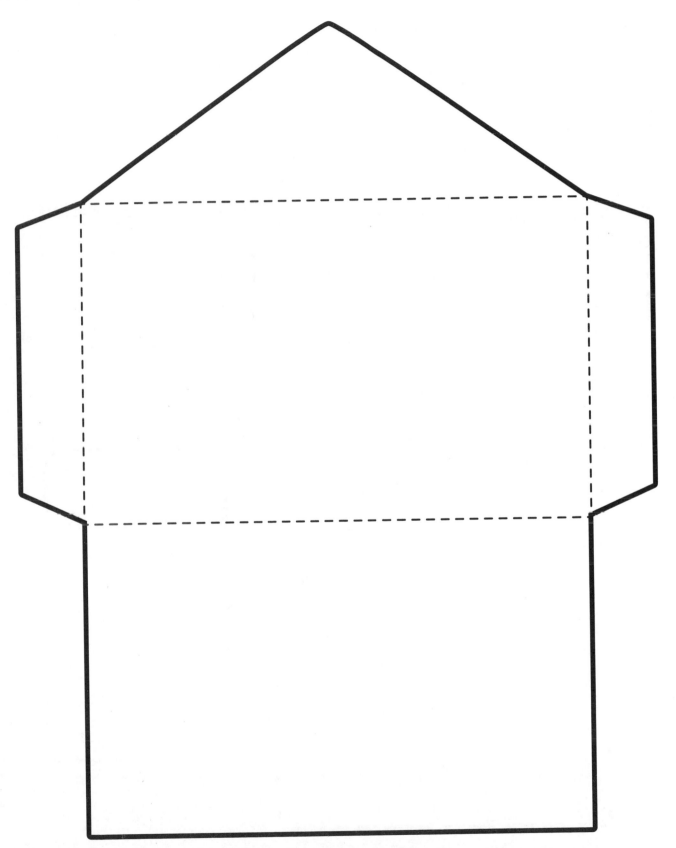

Pocket and Cards

Cut out the pocket on the solid lines. Fold over the front of the pocket. Then, apply glue to the tabs and fold them around the back of the pocket. Apply glue to the back of the pocket to attach it to a notebook page. Cut out the cards and store them in the envelope.

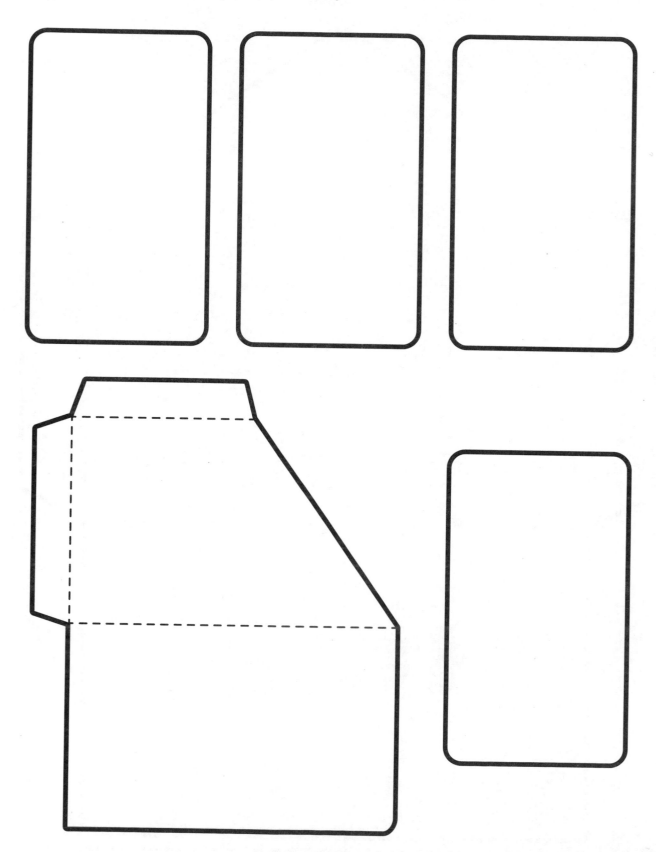

Six-Flap Shutter Fold

Cut out the shutter fold around the outside border. Then, cut on the solid lines to create six flaps. Fold the flaps toward the center. Apply glue to the back of the shutter fold to attach it to a notebook page.

If desired, this template can be modified to create a four-flap shutter fold by cutting off the bottom row. You can also create two three-flap books by cutting it in half down the center line.

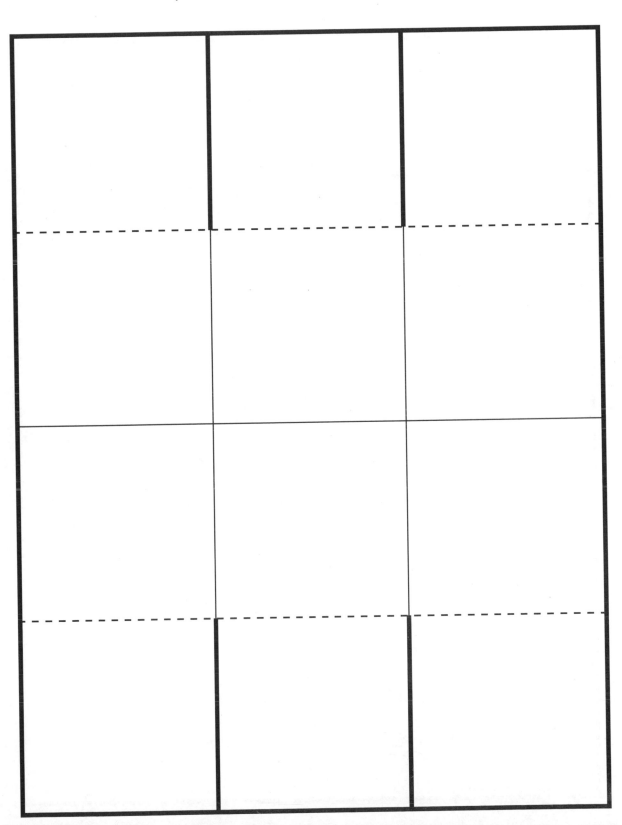

Eight-Flap Shutter Fold

Cut out the shutter fold around the outside border. Then, cut on the solid lines to create eight flaps. Fold the flaps toward the center. Apply glue to the back of the shutter fold to attach it to a notebook page.

If desired, this template can be modified to create two four-flap shutter folds by cutting off the bottom two rows. You can also create two four-flap books by cutting it in half down the center line.

Flap Book—Eight Flaps

Cut out the flap book around the outside border. Then, cut on the solid lines to create eight flaps. Apply glue to the back of the center section to attach it to a notebook page.

If desired, this template can be modified to create a six-flap or two four-flap books by cutting off the bottom row or two. You can also create a tall four-flap book by cutting off the flaps on the left side.

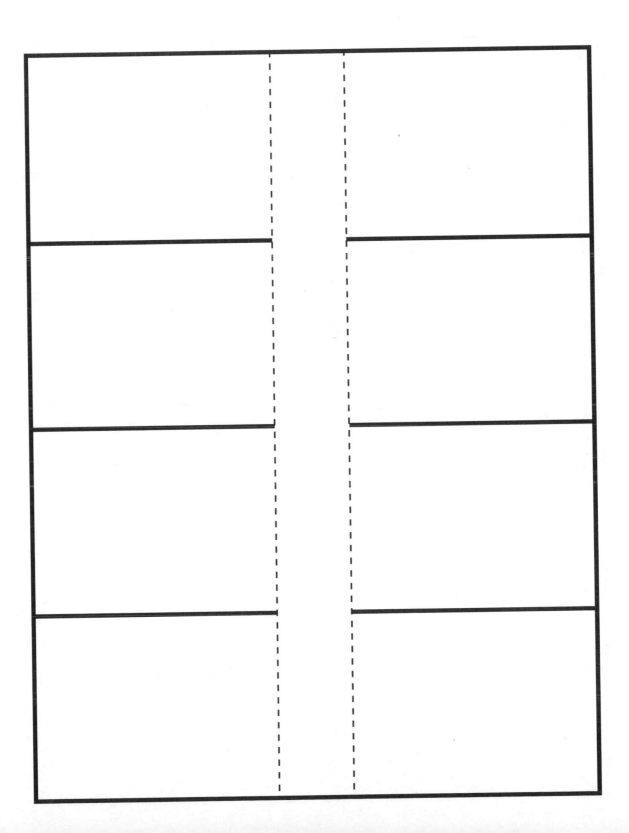

Flap Book—Twelve Flaps

Cut out the flap book around the outside border. Then, cut on the solid lines to create 12 flaps. Apply glue to the back of the center section to attach it to a notebook page.

If desired, this template can be modified to create smaller flap books by cutting off any number of rows from the bottom. You can also create a tall flap book by cutting off the flaps on the left side.

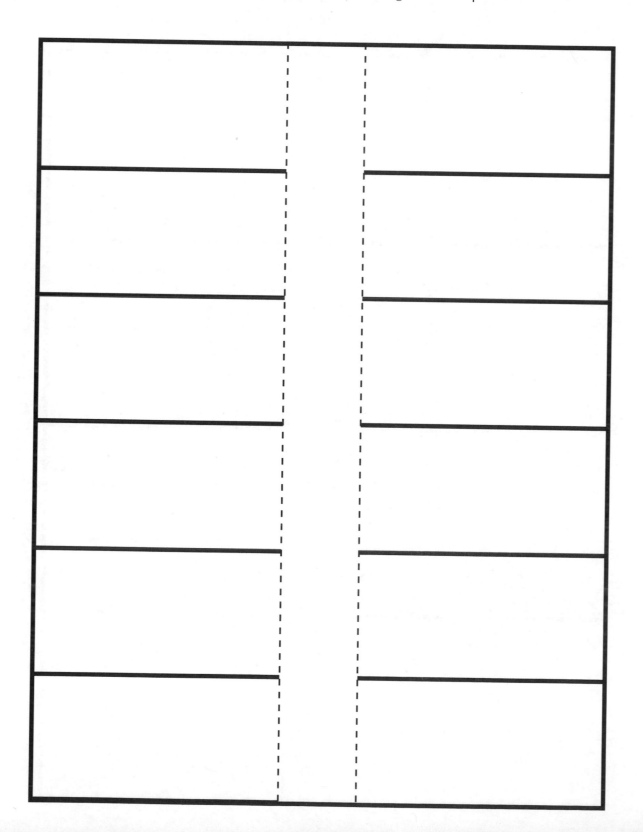

Shaped Flaps

Cut out each shaped flap. Apply glue to the back of the narrow section to attach it to a notebook page.

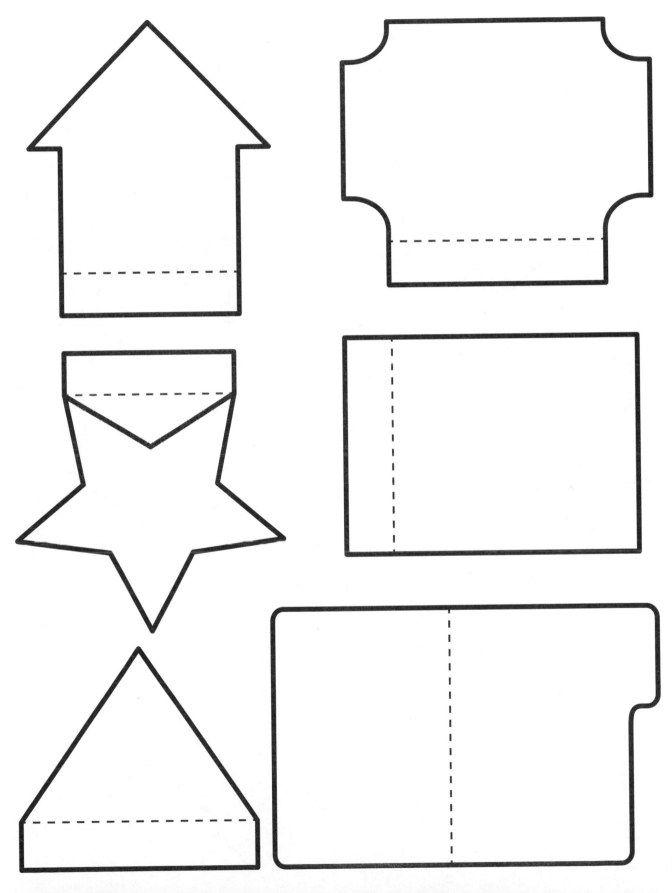

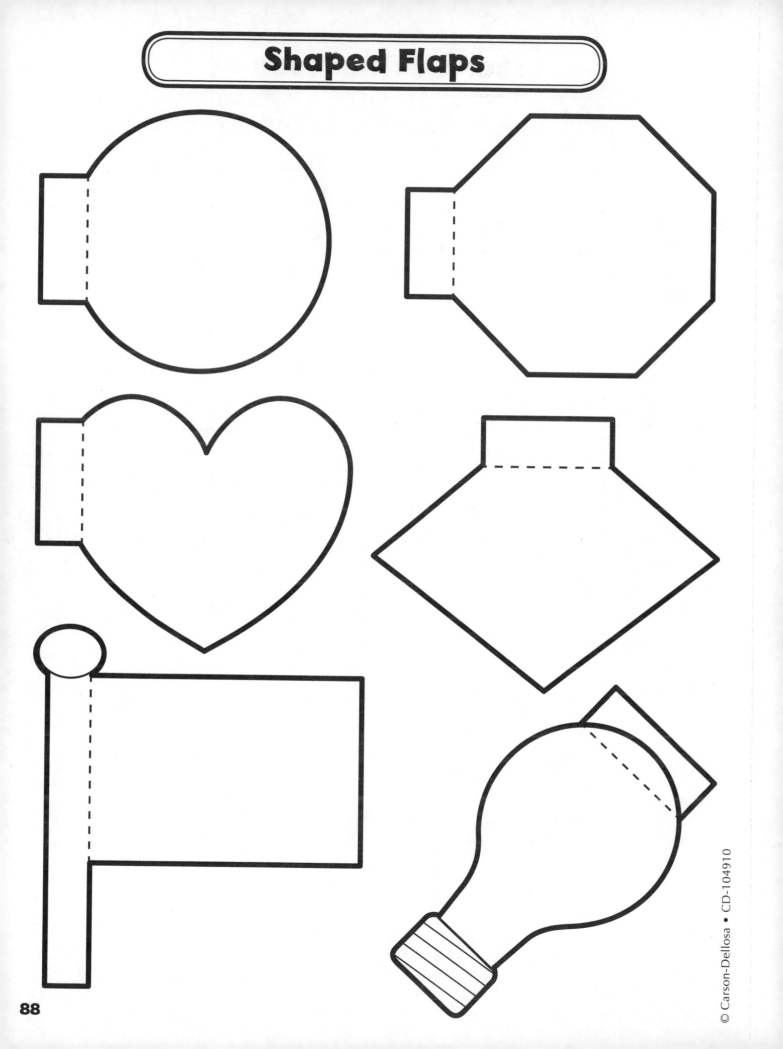

Interlocking Booklet

Cut out the booklet on the solid lines, including the short vertical lines on the top and bottom flaps. Then, fold the top and bottom flaps toward the center, interlocking them using the small vertical cuts. Apply glue to the back of the center panel to attach it to a notebook page.

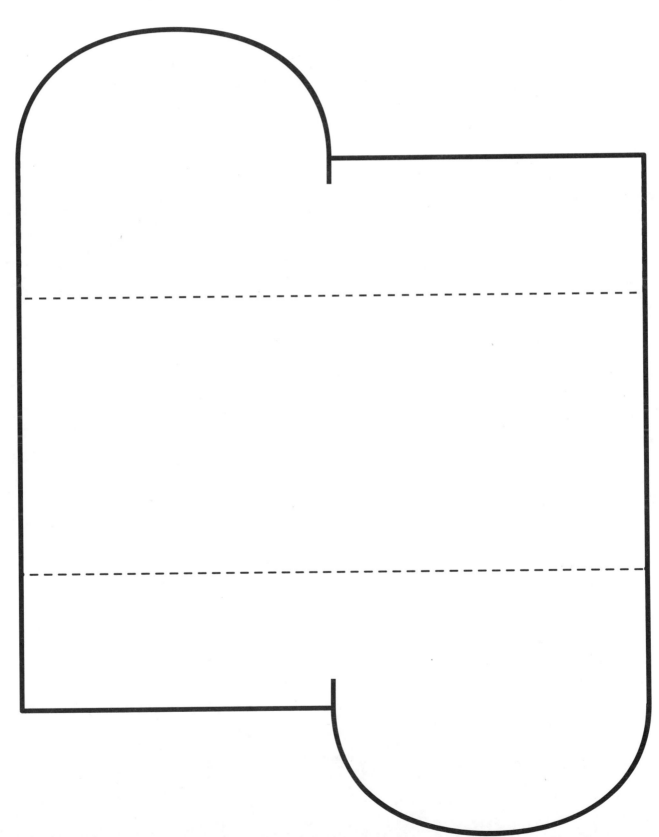

Four-Flap Petal Fold

Cut out the shape on the solid lines. Then, fold the flaps toward the center. Apply glue to the back of the center panel to attach it to a notebook page.

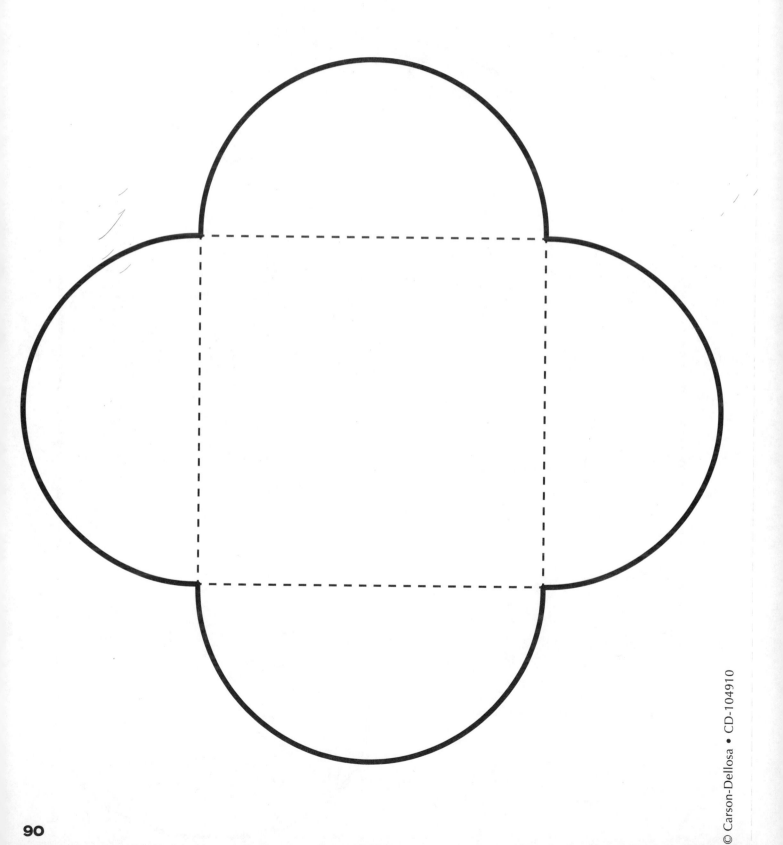

Six-Flap Petal Fold

Cut out the shape on the solid lines. Then, fold the flaps toward the center and back out. Apply glue to the back of the center panel to attach it to a notebook page.

Accordion Folds

Cut out the accordion pieces on the solid lines. Fold on the dashed lines, alternating the fold direction. Apply glue to the back of the last section to attach it to a notebook page.

You may modify the accordion books to have more or fewer pages by cutting off extra pages or by having students glue the first and last panels of two accordion books together.

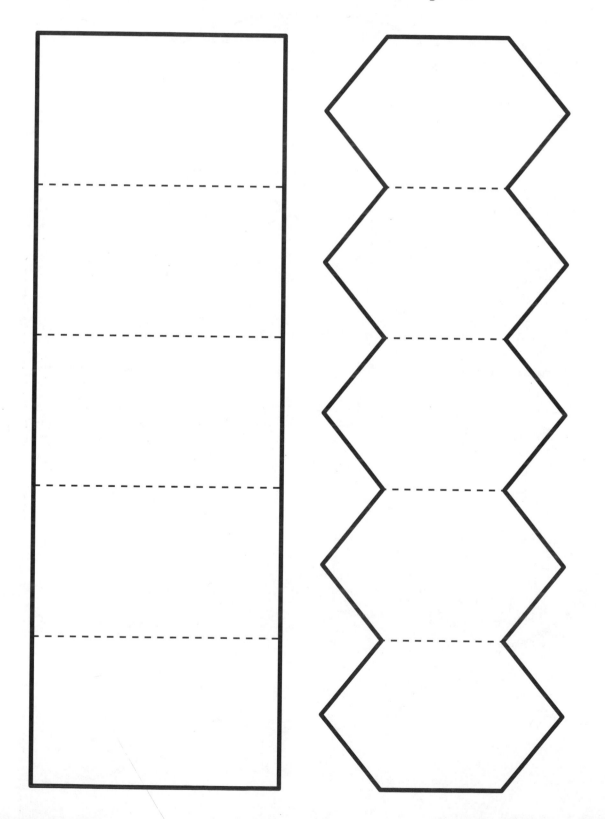

Accordion Folds

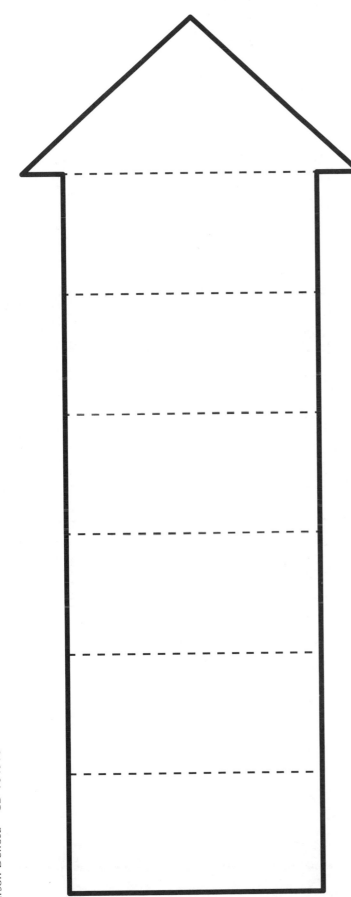

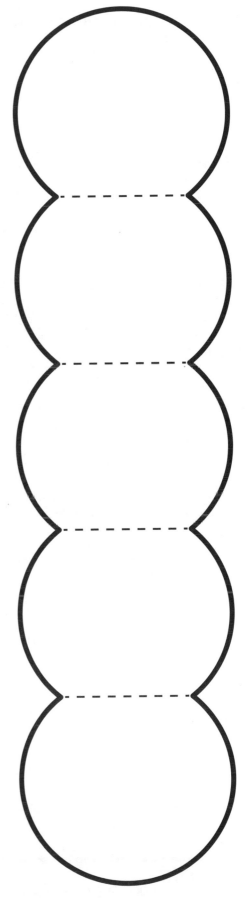

Clamshell Fold

Cut out the clamshell fold on the solid lines. Fold and unfold the piece on the three dashed lines. With the piece oriented so that the folds form an X with a horizontal line through it, pull the left and right sides together at the fold line. Then, keeping the sides touching, bring the top edge down to meet the bottom edge. You should be left with a triangular shape that unfolds into a square. Apply glue to the back of the triangle to attach the clamshell to a notebook page.

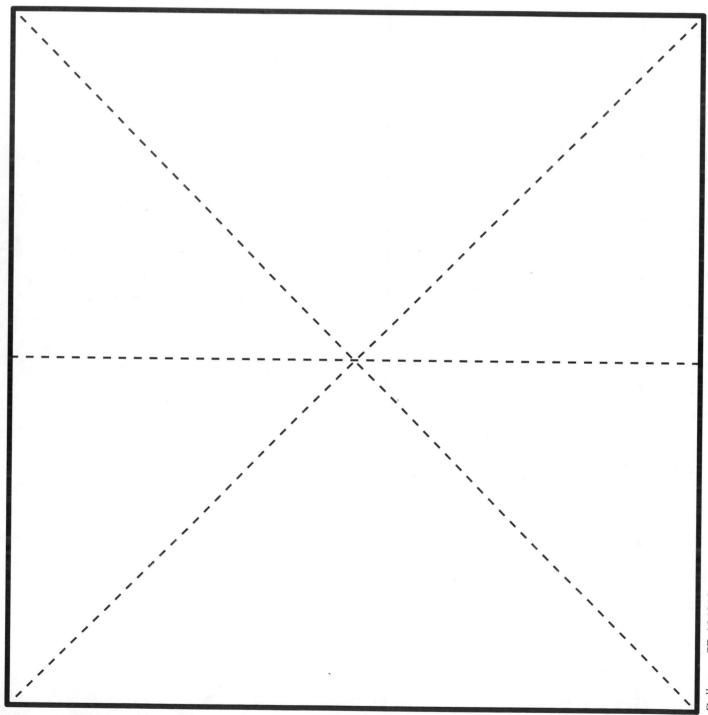

Puzzle Pieces

Cut out each puzzle along the solid lines to create a three- or four-piece puzzle. Apply glue to the back of each puzzle piece to attach it to a notebook page. Alternately, apply glue only to one edge of each piece to create flaps.

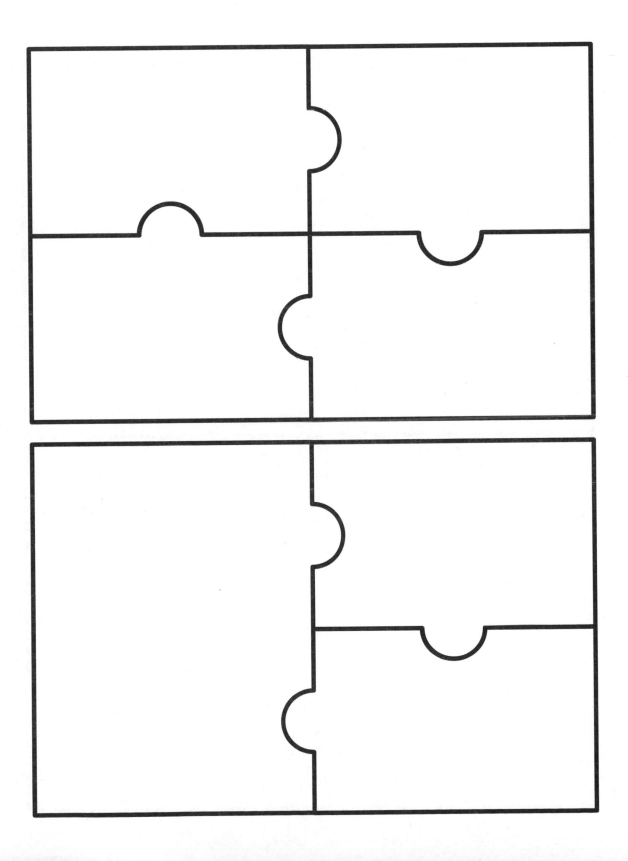

Flip Book

Cut out the two rectangular pieces on the solid lines. Fold each rectangle on the dashed lines. Fold the piece with the gray glue section so that it is inside the fold. Apply glue to the gray glue section and place the other folded rectangle on top so that the folds are nested and create a book with four cascading flaps. Make sure that the inside pages are facing up so that the edges of both pages are visible. Apply glue to the back of the book to attach it to a notebook page.

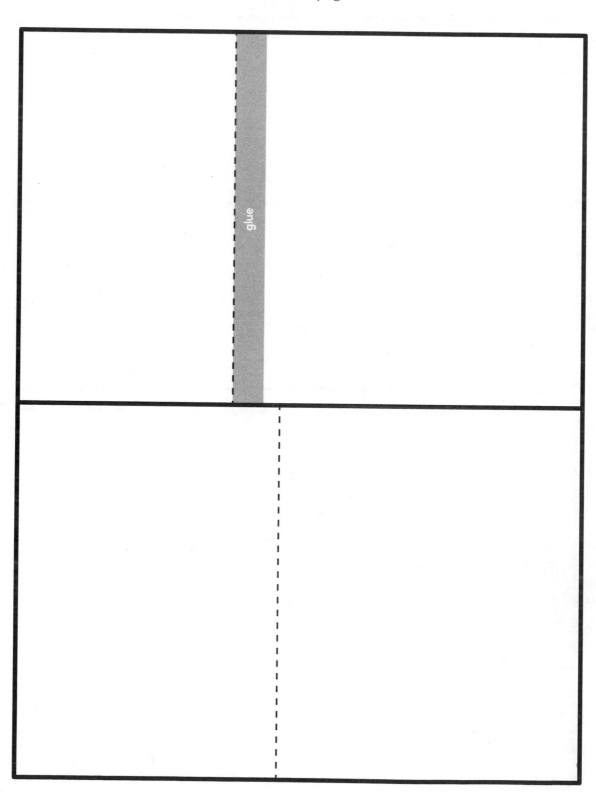